SUSTAINABLE INTERIOR DESIGN

CHLOE BULLOCK

RIBA Publishing

Sustainable Interior Design is printed on White Offset 350gsm and White Offset 120gsm paper, FSC. Papers Carbon Balanced by the World Land Trust. Printed with eco-friendly high-quality vegetable-based inks by Pureprint Group, the world's first carbon neutral printer.

Based on a formula developed by Mike Berners-Lee, author of *How Bad Are Bananas*, the author calculates the carbon impact value of this book to be an estimated 3.2k CO_2e.

FSC
www.fsc.org

MIX
Paper | Supporting
responsible forestry
FSC® C022913

© RIBA Publishing, 2024

Published by RIBA Publishing, 66 Portland Place, London, W1B 1AD

ISBN 9781914124990

British Library Cataloguing-in-Publication Data

A catalogue record for this book is available from the British Library.

Commissioning Editor: Liz Webster

Production: Marie Doinne

Designed and typeset by Studio Kalinka

Printed and bound by Pureprint Group Ltd

Cover design: Studio Kalinka

Illustrations: Elena Branch - @elenadrewthis

www.ribapublishing.com

Contents

Dedication
To my inspirational grandmothers

Acknowledgements

Sue Bullock
Ian Bullock
Paul Curtiss
Rob Beard
James Bullock
Charlotte Day
Sharon Anderson
Paul Lester
David Hall
Janet Curtiss
Karen Campbell
David Pannell
Sadie Miller Maggs
Jecks Stone
Anna Williamson
LuAnn Nigara
Nancy Ganzekaufer
Deborah Di Mare
Emma Payne
Jenny Barrett
Cat Fletcher
Clare Potter
Harriet Dean Orange
Steve Creed
David Greenfield
Martin Knox

Phillipa Bray
Jarvis Smith
Katie Hill
Safia Minney
Tim Etherington-Judge
Stephanie Jordan-Balmforth
Rachel Savage
Samantha Oakley
Rhodri Samuel
Lord Stone of Blackheath
Carole Cosgrove
Janey Lee Grace
Shauna Jordan
Jess Rad
Karen Stenning
Eleanor Mills
Rebecca Heaps
Aline Durr
Romy Rawlins
Leah Dawtrey
Darren Salerno
Gregory Medwin
John Espinosa
Jeff Hayward
Susie Rumbold
Dean Keyworth

Lori Pinkerton-Rolet
Katherine Elworthy
Lester Bennett
Rob Jones
Jo Percival
Sally Watkins
Catherine Leung
Mark Bell
Jason Lim
Sophie Tanner
Josie Lees
Vicky Schildkamp
Sonya Simmonds
Graeme Brooker
Jo Saady
Sean Garrick
Peter Buckfield
Rupert Mailand
Mitali Deypurkaystha
Star Khechara
Rachel Seri
Kevin Ball
Giulia Mori
Katie Proctor
Amy Snoekstra
Adam Bastock

Megan Wong
Stephen Choi
Susanne Conway
Neil Andrew
Carolyn Hayles
Bel Jacobs
Emma Hakansson
Delyth Fetherston-Dilke
Jen Gale
Laura Gelder-Robinson
Rebecca Kimber
Jane Davidson
Christiane Lellig
Rachael Pigg
Elinor Weekley
Catherine Coward
Estelle Levin-Nally
Gareth Mitchell
Jai Street
Dan Sherrard-Smith
Barbara Chandler
Declan Lowney
Paul Spendley

ATMOSPHERE

Quite simply, we could not exist without Earth's atmosphere. It gives us the oxygen we need to breathe, filters out harmful UV radiation from the Sun, and keeps our home planet at a habitable temperature.

Dr Sharon Ann Holgate, award-winning science writer and broadcaster, awarded the 2022 William Thomson Lord Kelvin Medal and Prize[1]

Gannets are found with flame retardant in their gut.[6]

Plastic is found in human lungs and blood.[5]

Birds are found to have ingested plastic.[2]

A heatwave in the UK in 2022 saw temperatures reaching a record 40°C and wildfires breaking out.[4]

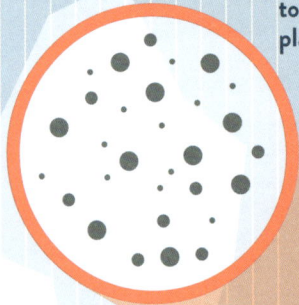

Air pollution is recorded as a medical cause of death for the first time in the UK, following a fatal asthma attack.[3]

Ambient air pollution and household air pollution is associated with 7 million premature deaths annually, worldwide. Household air pollution affects around 2.4 billion people globally, who are exposed to dangerous levels while using polluting open fires or simple stoves for cooking fuelled by kerosene, biomass (wood, animal dung and crop waste) and coal.[7]

Space junk and collisions on Earth are likely in the near future.[9]

NASA has reported the summer of 2023 as the hottest on record globally.[8]

Rainwater in the Tibetan Plateau and Antarctica has been found to contain 'forever chemicals' (PFAS/ per- and polyfluoroalkyl substances).[10]

EARTH

If oceans are the left lung of the Earth, rainforests are the right, generating around a fifth of the world's oxygen. They cover just 6% of the planet's surface and yet they support around two thirds of plant species and a quarter of insect species.

Natalie Fée, author, speaker and founder of UK-based plastic pollution campaign group City to Sea [11]

Soil health is depleted and there have been claims that there are less than 60 harvests left.[13]

Fire retardants have been found in the breast milk of women firefighters.[14]

Biophysical chemist Arlene Blum's cat, Midnight, developed hyperthyroid disease. Samples of her blood and house dust were sent to be tested. Midnight had very high levels of PBDEs (polybrominated diphenyl ethers) in her body and Blum's house dust contained 95 parts per million. Fire-retardant chemicals are believed to migrate out of furniture and then accumulate in house dust, food, animals and people.[17]

High levels of polychlorinated biphenyls (PCBs) have been found in the breast milk of Inuit women.[15]

Toxic chemicals have been found in the Arctic.[18]

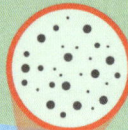

Killer whales have been found with flame retardant in their guts.[16]

Plastic has been found in the deepest point in the world – the Mariana Trench, in the western Pacific Ocean.[12]

Pollution in waterways and oceans is damaging blue carbon sinks and killing marine life.[19]

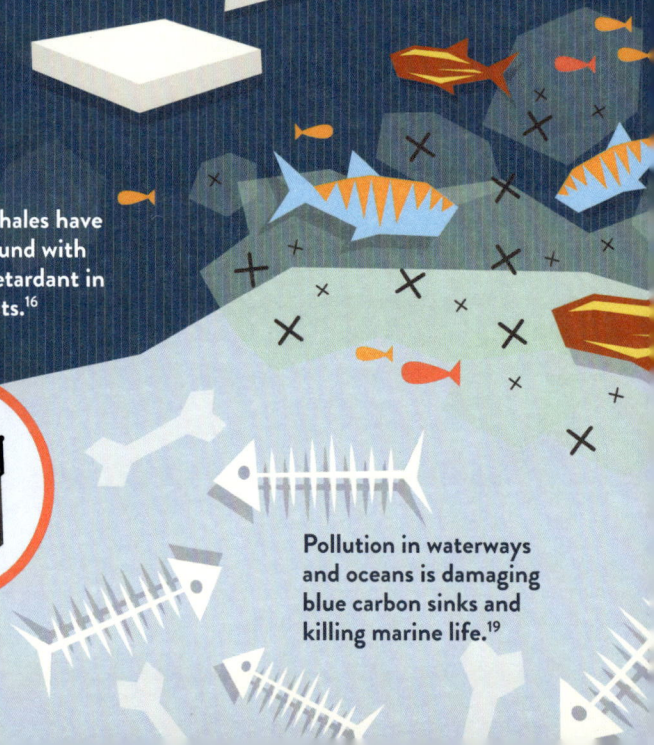

The displacement of Indigenous people and communities who are impacted by global boiling and other extreme weather conditions (flooding, coastal erosion, rising temperatures, pollution to waterways and air, and the inability to farm, fish and access clean water) is resulting in climate refugees.[20]

A global average of 69% of the planet's wildlife population has been wiped out since 1970.[23]

Animal agriculture is responsible for a large proportion of greenhouse gas emissions, plus deforestation and air pollution from the fires used to clear land.[24]

The Amazon rainforest – the 'lungs of the world' – has reached a tipping point. The rainforest has been a huge absorber of carbon dioxide (CO_2) and is now starting to emit CO_2, due to cattle ranching and livestock production. Around 80% of Amazon rainforest land in Brazil has been deforested.[26]

Paint is the largest source of microplastic in the world's oceans and waterways.[21]

Humans may be eating a credit card's worth of plastic each week.[25]

281652
16/07

Potable water - over 2 billion people live in water-stressed countries, which is expected to worsen as result of climate change and population growth.[27]

Some 14% of the world's coral was lost between 2009 and 2018.[22]

OCEANS AND WATERWAYS

When rain comes from the sky, it's the ocean touching you. When you breathe air, it's the ocean touching you. Our living ocean generates the oxygen, driving the great systems that keep us alive.

Dr Sylvia Earle, President and Chairman of Mission Blue/The Sylvia Earle Alliance; National Geographic Society Explorer in residence [28]

EARTH OVERSHOOT DAY

Earth Overshoot Day[29] is monitored globally and by country each year. While the Earth and its renewable resources stay the same, economies, populations and resource demands are increasing and are unsustainable. The date signifies the point in a year where we use more resources than the Earth can regenerate and we exceed our planetary boundaries.

Learning about this hugely important date each year really opened my eyes to the huge problems we face. These problems are brought home even more significantly when you look at the Earth Overshoot Day statistics for 1970, the year I was born. In this year, humanity almost reached the end of the calendar year before we used up the year's resources, falling short by one day. Less than six decades later, in 2022, humanity's demand on the planet reached the overshoot tipping point in July, with individual countries with high rates of consumption hitting their overshoot far earlier in the year. This ecological footprint is clear evidence of our global resource consumption rates.

United Nations projections predict a world population of 9.7 billion in 2050, more than 2.5 times more than in 1970.[30] The Earth's population clearly cannot sustain this growth. Nature's resources are not endless and cannot endlessly supply humans' exploitation of them – humanity is interdependent, and we need to work with nature's living systems.

While we are on the subject of the world since 1970, we have experienced the largest loss of the planet's wildlife population since the dinosaurs were wiped out, with an average global loss of 69% since 1970. This rapid wildlife extinction is directly connected to humans.

Oh yes, and to make these facts really relevant, it's reported that…

'WORLDWIDE, THE CONSTRUCTION INDUSTRY CONTRIBUTES TO:

50% OF ALL CLIMATE CHANGE,

40% OF DRINKING WATER POLLUTION,

23% OF AIR POLLUTION AND

50% OF LANDFILL WASTE.'[31]

Governments, industry and individuals: we all need to and can do more. The need for urgency is very present. We can no longer wait for others to initiate action.

Our design industry

Clients, designers, suppliers, manufacturers, craftspeople and supply chains – and our wider project teams: surveyors, architects, developers, investors, project managers, lighting designers, engineers, contractors, tradespeople, quantity surveyors, waste handlers, facilities managers, cleaners, maintenance technicians – are all stakeholders in the creation of an interior and its lifespan. We need to examine how we work, and we all have areas we can improve upon to lessen our impact. Everything needs to become more multi-directional in the world of working sustainably. Instead of simply fulfilling a client's brief, designers find themselves with opportunities to influence the stakeholders around them, including our clients. We can encourage clients to follow a more conscious approach to their projects, and conversely clients can encourage designers, too, based on their own values or desire to follow a framework or certification. Clients depend on designers for our expertise and experience. We depend on our suppliers to supply us with goods that are reliable, good quality and that demonstrate our creativity.

Interior designers are very much part of a marketing machine promoting consumption, whether we like it or not, and we have a great opportunity to demand transparency, evaluate what is being used and involve clients in more informed decision-making. Our suppliers will respond to the needs of the market. Some are innovative and proactive and are already there and ready to support us. Some are slower to respond, perhaps less agile and are waiting for the lead from legislation. Predicted climate events are happening sooner than scientists have anticipated. There isn't time to wait for legislation. We are all stakeholders so we all need to act with responsibility, urgency and with positive agency, within our remit and influence and, where we possibly can, outside of it.

Many designers have routinely woven sustainability into how they work. To some, however, this adds a new layer to their already complex role. This book will demystify what sustainability means and why it is important that it becomes the norm for our industry, now and not in the future. The book will hopefully also spur you on and guide you to work in a better way for the health of nature, people and the planet. I will break down the many approaches to creating a sustainable interior, looking at the materials, specifications and processes required to design in this problem-solving way, whether driven by ethics, values or health.

Admittedly, when working on the net-zero action plan for my own company, my gut reaction was to retire early in order to avoid it! However, I feel strongly that interior designers are extremely capable and highly trained problem-solvers – we're not just followers of fashions and trends. Designing is not shopping. Specifying doesn't mean that only virgin materials are used. We have a huge opportunity to change that approach and also to influence those around us in the project team and our clients. Adding 'working sustainably' into the mix is just one more layer to how interior designers work. It's another problem to solve. Designers can work creatively and beautifully, with a reduced impact, and this is completely achievable. The main aim of this book is to demonstrate beautiful and sustainable spaces that will inspire and educate us all to work better at all scales and sizes.

As designers, we often seem to be stuck in a repetition of the familiar (materials, processes and tradespeople), combined with client pleasing in order for project after project to be completed and paid for. Then on to the next, without any thought for the spaces post occupancy. We often miss the opportunity to learn and improve for future projects by evaluating previous ones.

We now need to play our part in the pushing of boundaries and work outside of our comfort zones in all the directions which we have an influence upon. We can rethink and relearn new ways of working and different methodologies, while lessening our impact on the planet, people and the animal kingdom.

I have so many questions to ask our industry, on all scales. Many seem to be about disconnections.

How have we become so disconnected from nature that we can't see the consequences of our industry upon it? Can't we see how everything is interdependent?

Why are we so disconnected from the impact of our work? Designers are the link connecting supply chains to clients. We are too disengaged from our responsibilities around conscious and responsible sourcing and specifying. *Why don't we connect more to the materials, processes and people involved? Our clients need our guidance; isn't it our duty to know more so we can lead and guide them?*

Why do members of project teams, including interior designers, work in isolation so much? Collaboration with a wider project team as early as possible is proving to efficiently and successfully deliver lower-impact projects. *Why don't we work in partnership, together?*

Interior design combines art with science: beauty and function. But it's also about how to improve the human experience of spaces. As designers, we're increasingly aware of the impact of the spaces we create on users, both positive and negative, as well as the impact of those spaces on health, emotions and experience. The interior design industry has a significant impact on the environment through manufacturing and the supply chain. Materials and products that we routinely specify use carbon, extraction, drilling, mining, natural resources, water, toxic chemicals and exploitation of people and animals.

Designers have a huge opportunity and responsibility to improve by consciously avoiding materials and processes that impact on people and the planet, while also meeting our clients' briefs.

The Word *Sustainable*

I'm using the word *sustainable* as a hook because it's become so familiar to us all. It's not a word I like, but I will keep using it. What it means is maintaining a level of consumption without depleting resources or causing damage to the environment and the Earth's cohabitants — both people and the animal kingdom. We know that maintaining this level is not nearly enough in response to the crises we face. As permaculture designer Matthew Lynch put it so well in his TEDx talk:

> 'If I tell you 'My wife and I have a sustainable relationship,' what am I saying about the quality of our relationship? Why don't we use words like flourishing or nurturing or regenerative? Or what if I were to tell you my relationship with my wife was 'freaking awesome'?! If we were to start talking like this, what kind of world could we create?'[32]

Our solutions must exceed sustainability. They need to be a process of regenerative sustainability where a wider connection to the environment and nature is made. I love this quote from regenerative development expert Dr Dominque Hes:

> 'Give a man a fish and he will eat for a day. Teach him how to fish and he will eat for a lifetime,' well, unless the fish run out. Regenerative development turns that around and says, 'Teach a man to love the ocean and they'll both thrive.'[33]

Sustainability has many different interpretations, viewpoints and definitions. I'm not sure when I first noticed the word sustainable used in the interior design industry. I certainly don't remember 'sustainable design' being used to describe how we were working when I was a retail designer for Anita Roddick's values-driven ethical business The Body Shop International's headquarters from the mid-1990s. The principles of triple bottom line of people, planet and profit, however, were very much present in all decisions, and sustainable development was clearly the company's focus. Sustainable development was in everything the company did — and still does. At time of writing, The Body Shop International is owned by Natura &Co, the world's largest B Corporation.[34] Sustainable development is a process of continuous improvement. It's very much more than simply 'sustainable'. We are hearing the term *sustainable* in our daily lives more and more, from fashion, to food, to travel. Yet *sustainable* is a term many are moving away from – there is a need for urgency due to the climate and ecological breakdown we face. With global boiling happening faster than scientists have anticipated, maintaining the current level is just not enough to do in response.

In their book *Cradle to Cradle: Remaking the Way We Make Things*, William McDonough and Michael Braungart stated:

'As long as human beings are regarded as 'bad', zero is a good goal. But to be less bad is to accept things as they are, to believe that poorly designed, dishonourable, destructive systems are the best humans can do. This is the ultimate failure of the 'be less bad' approach: a failure of the imagination. From our perspective, this is a depressing vision of our species' roles in the world. What about an entirely different model? What would it mean to be 100% good?'[35]

Designers in the industry are at many different stages of sustainable design. 'Less bad' would be where you'd have generally found me up until a few years ago, unless I had a client whose values and brief married up directly with mine. Many of us aren't even at 'less bad' yet – but there is now such urgency for us all to improve. We need to look even further to the regenerative version of sustainability, where we replenish and restore through our work.

Being 'less bad' is no longer enough as we face evidence of humans' impact on nature and we reach such significant ecological tipping points. If we look at just one indicator, consider the Amazon rainforest, which has been a carbon sink, a huge absorber of a quarter of the planet's CO_2. It is now starting to emit more CO_2 than it absorbs.[36] Why? The obvious reason is deforestation, which is happening rapidly for logging, mining and land clearing for animal agriculture and soya production, some of which feeds those animals and some is exported along with the timber and beef, releasing more CO_2. Bad enough, but that land clearing is achieved using fires, which then increases the temperature

on a long-term basis, as the soot absorbs sunlight. Cattle emit methane, also a greenhouse gas which increases temperature. The land is drying out, so floods are more frequent and so are wildfires, which are occurring at the highest rate on record. This whole natural system is misfunctioning.[37] The design industry uses these materials, as do many other industries.

As designers, we need to be more inquisitive and challenging of the materials and processes we use. We need to embed sustainability at the core of the brief, whether or not it's requested by the client. We may need to challenge briefs or even whether whole projects should happen at all, and actively encourage clients and the wider project team to achieve better within their remits, too.

In this book, I will explore what the many project goals for a sustainable interior design might be, whether the motive comes from you as a designer or your client. We'll look at varying scales, from finishes and furniture to spaces and buildings. I will also show how a sustainable solution is likely to improve health and wellbeing. I will explore the threads of sustainability and cover some of the many approaches there are to a sustainable interior. I see these approaches as useful tools to inspire and engage our industry, as well as our clients and other stakeholders in our projects.

Let me inspire you with some approaches to creating an interior design. In the following chapters, I have categorised some of the routes, demonstrating that sustainability can be creative, aesthetically beautiful and joyful, too – so there are no excuses not to design more consciously. I hope the following chapters will energise you as much as they have me.

Q **explore**

Calculate your own ecological footprint at
www.footprintcalculator.org

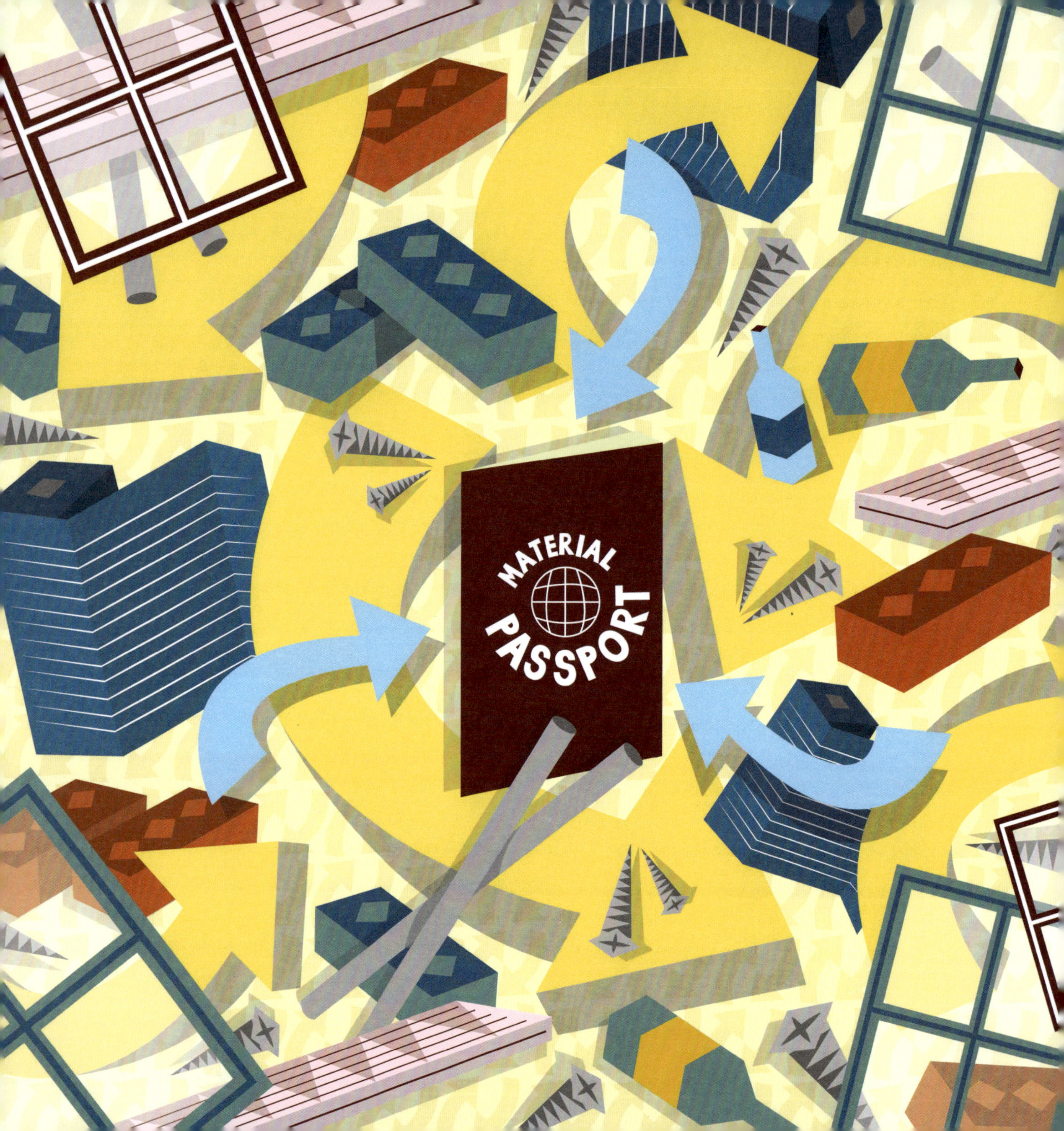
MATERIAL
PASSPORT

1

Reuse

The greenest building is one that already exists. The purest form of reuse is to use again as is, with minimal demolition or addition. There are many interpretations of the reuse approach, and *50/50 Words for Reuse – A Minifesto*,[1] by Graeme Brooker, professor and head of interior design at the Royal College of Art, illustrates 51 of them intricately.

Reuse requires appreciation of the beauty of 'aged'. Signs of a previous use, perhaps in the form of patina, cracks or shadows, often indicate the previous life. The Japanese life and aesthetic philosophy of *wabi-sabi*, from the 16th century (or possibly earlier), encapsulates this acceptance of the beauty of imperfection. *Kintsugi*, the ancient Japanese art of reuse through a visible repair in gold or silver, honours a memory, while enhancing its beauty.

Fast-forward to reuse today. Buildings are increasingly being regarded as material banks, storing materials during their use phase. This tracking, tracing and logging of material resources while in use is also referred to as Materials as a Service, depending on the ownership status. Each component part is designed for disassembly and traceability, with a radio frequency identification label linking to a digital document: a materials passport, which ensures materials are tracked and provides assurance of performance. This combination enables the valuable resources within to be easily identified and kept at their highest value for as long as possible once dismantled at end-of-life stage. Demolition as we have known it – the wrecking and smashing of potential resources to their lowest-value rubble – has to be avoided. Instead, we can see a shift to urban mining – or 'mining the Anthropocene'[2] as circular economy architect Duncan Baker-Brown calls it – for building materials, finishes, furniture, fixtures and equipment. All can be assisted by materials passports. Fast-forward again to the future, where supply chains are fully transparent thanks to an added level of blockchain technology, where encrypted data can be applied securely to materials. This technology will enable a truly circular economy where everything can be trusted without uncertainty.

Apart from the obvious benefits of the reduced use of resources, reusing materials can evoke memories and add character, making an interior familiar and playful. In a time when materials and energy costs are rising, coupled with supply chain issues and scarcity, I can't think of a better approach to a sustainable interior – where necessity meets creativity without further negative impact being needed.

Intercontinental Khao Yai Resort
Nakhon Ratchasima, Thailand

' This is the first time such a big hotel operator backs upcycling on such a big scale. I hope that more follow suit and follow the lesser-tread path of major upcycling and recycling, as it brings huge appeal to any project and so much character.'

Bill Bensley[3]

Bangkok-based designer, architect and landscape gardener Bill Bensley has reused heritage train carriages as guest accommodation for the railway-inspired Intercontinental Khao Yai Resort, Thailand. This is a beautiful example of reuse, evoking memories of when the region was a gateway for rail travel from Khao Yai's former station.

The resort sits on the edge of the forested Khao Yai National Park – a very special place which is a UNESCO World Heritage Site. For part of the resort, Bensley was faced with the need to have small-footprint hotel buildings that would fit between wooded areas and avoid damage to tree drainage. His idea to use repurposed train carriages provided a nostalgic and sensitive solution. It also perfectly fits Bensley's own company's ethos. He is a nature lover and conservationist and has a love of combining storytelling (sometimes fictitious!) with upcycling and using locally and consciously sourced crafts, materials and antiques to create experiences for visitors.

Bensley and his Bangkok-based multidisciplinary creative team set to work. Carriages were sourced and recovered from all over Thailand for the project. Many had been neglected for more than 50 years. A few had trees which had taken root inside them, so serious restoration work was needed, although Bensley has left sections of the beautiful root system on show as a reminder of Mother Nature's attempt to reclaim. The carriages form 19 luxury suites and villas

1.1 Designer, architect and landscape gardener Bill Bensley and team members convert a heritage train carriage into guest accommodation.

with plunge pools, a tearoom, bistro, cocktail bar and spa where guests are transported back in time.

While the condition of some of the carriages has meant more of a rebuild than pure reuse, Bensley's projects all follow his guidelines set out in his 'Sensible Sustainable Solutions' White Paper.[4] He also uses the Leadership in Energy and Environmental Design (LEED) green building framework, although his projects have not been officially certified. Identifying the need to collaborate and share knowledge, Bensley wrote the open-source 'Sensible sustainable solutions' White Paper for the hotel industry after 30 years in the sector, to recognise the industry's part in climate change and encourage more conscious and responsible design, drawing on the lessons he had learnt on building and running hotels sustainably.

The White Paper outlines 16 suggestions, covering three core pillars impacting people, animals and the planet:

1   Build with a purpose – offer experiences, educate guests and employees. Work with and support the local community. Champion environmental issues, wildlife protection and conservation.

2   Operate locally – meaning a focus on local sourcing of products and food, even using food grown in the grounds of the hotel. Responsibly select locally sourced materials and carefully recycle locally.

3   Create respectfully – respect the land and work with nature, sun and daylight. Source carefully. Preserve and minimise energy use. Be careful in your use of material resources, and aim for minimal waste.

Bensley states in the White Paper:

Luxury is DEAD. I am done with designing lavish hotels just to put heads on beds. Every hospitality project that we have on the drawing boards right now has a purpose and a candle to light. Those of us in hospitality – be it designers, owners or operators – have the power of reaching thousands of people through our hotels and spreading this message of purpose. We should shoulder more responsibility concerning issues such as education, clean, accessible water, alternative energy, energy consumption, food waste, wildlife protection and conservation. Let's all lose the greenwash and do something real.[5]

This project takes Bensley a step closer to his dream of designing a 100% recycled hotel, which he regularly pitches to his clients – maybe even using an aeroplane or grounded ship.

1.4 The completed interior of a salvaged carriage, fully fulfilling the brief for evoking the golden age of train travel. This carriage fits in a bedroom with en-suite in the challenging footprint of 2.5m by 30m.

1.5 A guest room with bunk beds.

1.6 The refurbished Tea Carriage.

FACTS

Client: Intercontinental Hotel Group

Interior design: Bill Bensley

Completion: December 2022

Gross internal floor area: each carriage 75m^2

Visit: InterContinental Khao Yai Resort, 262, Pong Talong Sub-District, Pak Chong District, Nakhon Ratchasima 30450, Thailand, www.ihg.com/intercontinental/hotels/gb/en/khao-yai

Opposite:
1.2 Ficus trees had taken root on the roof of this carriage and almost completely enveloped it. The carriage was renovated and reused as a spa treatment room for the resort.

1.3 Renovated carriages ready for guests.

1.7 LocHal's 'stair tribune' – the wide steps that connect the ground, first and second floors – sits behind the café and entrance in the grand hall of the depot section. The curtains (on the left of the photo) can be used to separate the central section of the building. The main LocHal signage which sits on top of the café's servery module, can be seen from outside.

LocHal Library

Tilburg, Netherlands

Six enormous textile walls – in effect curtains – each measuring 15.5m high and 50m wide – were woven and made by TextielLab, the professional workspace of the TextielMuseum in Tilburg. An idea they conceived together with design studio Inside Outside, the monumental curtains form the adaptable interiors of LocHal, a former NS Dutch Rail locomotive repair shed built in 1932, which is now Tilburg's multi-award-winning city library. These curtains have transparent sections and cutouts forming windows and door openings. All designed, developed and made to conform to fire-retardant regulations, they can fold and unfold to meet different use requirements thanks to computer-controlled rails. Very little else has been added to the building's structure except suspended lighting. The textile walls are a most impressive project-within-a-project, and a creative way to treat this huge space, while referencing Tilburg's textile-producing heritage within one of NS Dutch Rail's sites – also a key part of the city's past. The multiuse public library sits within Tilburg's modernised station district and is a beautiful example of an adaptive reuse strategy – the use of an existing building for a new purpose. The LocHal building is home to the Midden-Brabant Library, the cultural institution Kunstloc Brabant, the regional culture and creative investment fund Brabant C and the Seats2meet co-working spaces. There are three sections to the original shed interior: the crane lane, the boiler repair shop and the depot.

The building is even home to a rescued glass dome structure from a 200-seat musical hall, which was bought from the Beurs van Berlage conference centre in Amsterdam for €1 after it was on the shortlist to be demolished.

Original features have been preserved. When adding to the scheme, the 'found' colours have been replicated throughout, taken from the original but worn colours of the pipes servicing the shed structure. Flaking paint has been left as is; patinas are appreciated. Any new material additions have been thoughtfully added in steel, timber and glass to blend with the original materials. Even the chairs and tables from the previous city library building were reused.

There are so many variations in scale of use within the shed building. These vary from large events in the great hall auditorium, to workshops and quiet working. Architects Mecanoo have reused the

1.8 Stage platforms, made from old damaged library books, double as gathering places with multiple levels and cushioned sections.

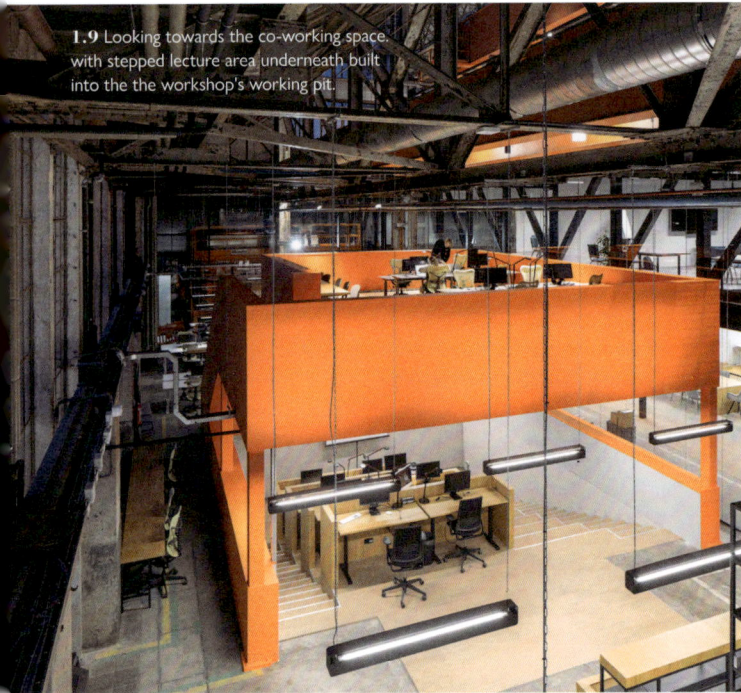

1.9 Looking towards the co-working space, with stepped lecture area underneath built into the the workshop's working pit.

1.10 The old tracks within the building have been kept and cleverly utilised to move three 'train' tables around the space. These tables can be used outside on the square for events, to extend the bar, to form a stage or to link to the stairs to form a catwalk.

working pit feature in the boiler repair workshop by adding furniture above it, utilising the stepped area for lectures and presentations, with a co-working area on top.

LocHal Library is a very comfortable building for users. Minimal heating and cooling has been added. The glazing has been replaced with solar-control double glazing to keep heat gain to a minimum, coupled with openings in the roof to let hot air flow out. When temperatures drop, the people are heated rather than the space. The 'stair tribune' seating has underfloor heating in the treads, heating where people sit. Smaller rooms have user-led independent temperature controls. External doorways are heated. A lower-energy displacement ventilation system was installed to pump fresh air, which warms up inside and rises.

Daylight is optimised thanks to the huge glass façade and restored roof lights. When lighting has been added, it's low energy, specified to suit the space and comfort for users. Some of the lighting was reused from the previous library. The interior is currently home to the world's largest circular-economy chandelier, with lamps made from 10,000 post-consumer PET bottles by local circular-economy initiative van Petnaar Pret.

Noise levels were modelled to enable Arup to produce a comfortable acoustic design for the varying activity spaces, ensuring the study spaces are quiet while the café is bustling and busy. The building is energy efficient, too, powered by 1,278 solar photovoltaic panels on its huge roof (the size of seven football pitches), producing enough electricity to power 80 households each year.

The central 'street' has industrial columns with workstation counters added to them. This crane lane, which cuts through three floors of the interior, is lined with plants and trees in huge planters made from repurposed floorboards from old train carriages.

Multifunction meeting spaces and laboratories are dotted around the shed with various uses – including gaming, local history, food, dialogue and learning languages. The Game Lab features recycled TV circuit boards used as decoration. Inside the Time Lab – the local

1.11 The central 'street'.   1.12 The children's library vibrantly references the local fairy-tale theme park, Efteling, with giant books and pencils as room dividers and bookcases, all sitting on the unchanged floor from the building's first use as a workshop.

history space – is a clock wall consisting of all the original clocks from workspaces in the shed. The reused clocks are connected and powered by the 'mother clock'. The Digi Lab is a space for inventors of all ages, and is used for learning about virtual reality, 3D printing, building games programming and creating open-source applications and hardware.

A more recent addition is inside the CityBalkon – a glazed space which spans a whole 60m elevation of the top floor of the building, with views across the city. It's the perfect location for a winter-garden greenhouse, where the lush, plant-filled space is used by local community initiatives to promote and learn about biodiversity and the growing of plants and food.

I visited in the day, but at night the front elevation of the shed becomes a lantern which beckons you in from outside. It's very much the cultural centre of the city: a place to meet, learn, study, cook, play, make and watch. One can't help thinking this exciting, highly accessible and well-loved public building interior is better for being in a reused structure that had an entirely different previous use. There are so many quirks and thoughtful touches that make it far more fun and unique for its users. It has many references that ground the reused structure to Tilburg's past and remind users of the building's history through thoughtful reused elements on all scales, and the addition of new elements. This thriving building is evidently well loved and used by the community. It's a huge adaptive reuse success story.

1.13 Mecanoo cleverly designed wayfinding signage using reused platform signs, with graphics in the same style as a reminder of the train connection.

1.14 The Word Lab is a bookcase-lined reading room, where the bookcases cover the ceiling as well (made from worn-out and damaged books). It's a perfect space for lovers of language, literature and creative writing.

FACTS

Client: LocHal

Interior design: Mecanoo Architects

Interior concept and textiles: Inside Outside and TextielMuseum

Architect: Civic Architects, Braaksma & Roos Architectenbureau and Inside Outside/Petra Blaisse

Sustainability/structural/mechanical/acoustic/ lighting/fire-safety consultant: Arup

Completion: December 2018, opened January 2019

Year of original construction: 1932

Gross internal floor area: 7,000m², including 1,300m² of offices

Visit: LocHal, Burgemeester Brokxlaan 1000, 5041 SG Tilburg, Netherlands, www.lochal.nl

Regene Office

Yokohama, Japan

While multidisciplinary design studio NOSINGER was preparing to relocate to its new office space in Chinatown, in Yokohama, Japan, lead designer Eisuke Tachikawa visited the new office while the former tenant was putting it back to its 'skeleton state', as required by Japanese law. He was faced with a two-tonne pile of distorted light-gauge steel wall studs and fixings that had been stripped from the interior.

For the NOSINGER collective, who describes itself as a 'social design activist that drives social change towards a more hopeful future', the pile represented an opportunity and a possibility. Having worked with waste as materials in the past, the team took charge of the perceived 'waste' from the demolition contractor and set about reusing it in their new office. Along with circular-economy consultants Zenloop and members of Keio University's Graduate School of Media Design, who it has partnered with before, it produced a thought-provoking spatial design based on reuse.

The project's new aim was to show how minimal the impact of a design concept could be, simply by appreciation for the materials and a creative approach to their reuse in a completely different way. The team had been disturbed by the construction industry's enormous, documented waste and high greenhouse gas emissions (CO_2e), produced both in Japan and globally.

1.16 The dismantled extrusions deemed as waste became decorative surface finishes, with the addition of recycled industrial aluminium foil and tiles made from fired waste materials.

1.17 The office in use.

The Regene Office template demonstrates how these commonly used construction elements found in site waste can be reused aesthetically and effectively as an interior material resource.

To reuse on site in this way is high on the value hierarchy, although to reuse in the original form again would be higher. This strategy for on-site upcycling of commonly used elements of construction waste showcases an innovative approach which retains the resources used in manufacturing and disposal that would otherwise be downcycled in value, using energy to transport and recycle. The office is now a base for advising industries on recycling, through design and consulting. NOSINGER hopes it will inspire others to value and use these recovered resources as interior decoration.

FACTS

Client, interior design: NOSINGER

Circular-Economy consultants: Zenloop

Lighting: Takeden

Completion: May 2021

Year of original construction: 1991

Gross internal floor area: 161.88m^2

1.18 The distorted steel fixings from the interior of the Regene Office.

KITCHEN FOR LIFE

Madrid, Spain

Kitchens are one of the most expensive furniture additions to a residential interior. They are also the area of great unnecessary waste. Two and a half million tonnes of kitchen furniture is discarded in the European Union each year. Most is landfilled or incinerated.[6]

It seems that kitchens are also the expression of the taste of the owners: a status symbol, even. Kitchens are often very personalised to the client and not bought to appeal to a future house buyer. There's certainly some psychology going on here. There's also evidence that post-purchase kitchen regrets are due to poor design.[7]

There are companies who carefully dismantle kitchens to resell. There are also companies who make beautiful doors to common sizes which give carcasses a longer life. However, kitchens are still so often on the list to be completely replaced by new owners of a house, rather than being the reason for buying a house. I have first-hand experience of this. I've seen my own newly installed, well-designed and inoffensive kitchen ripped out and replaced by the new owners, and then ripped out and replaced again only four to five years later by the next owners. No adaptation or tweaking happened; judging by the skip outside, it was a complete redesign and refit in both cases.

Kitchens are usually modular, dry fitted and often extremely durable. They are demountable and reusable, with the exception of any site customisation. A challenge to easy reuse can be the services, worktops and integrated appliance design, but reuse is still possible.

In the UK, the cost to dismantle is often similar to the cost of destruction, and taking a kitchen to landfill costs around £850 + VAT for the average-sized kitchen, according to Helen Lord, of Rehome (formerly the Used Kitchen Exchange). One in four kitchens replaced in the UK are under four years old.[8] So why do so many go directly to landfill far sooner than their functional end of life?

1.19 Kitchen and island with an invisible induction hob.

1.20 A Kitchen for Life drawer unit.

1.21 Paula Rosales.

1.22 The modular storage can be used as a room divider.

I have often heard clients saying they wish they could have brought their previous kitchen with them to their new home. Spanish brand KITCHEN FOR LIFE seems to have broken through the kitchen-buying psychology with its clever designs that are attractive, while also being healthy and without toxins, made from reduced materials, demountable and able to be reused easily many times, whether or not by the original purchaser.

Madrid-based architect Paula Rosales, of more&co, the architectural practice behind KITCHEN FOR LIFE, couldn't understand why a kitchen would stay in your old home when you moved. 'Why take the sofa with you but not the kitchen, when the kitchen cost you ten times more?' she wondered.

Rosales and her team at more&co developed KITCHEN FOR LIFE, an innovative modular, metal-framed furniture storage concept, which has broken the mould of the traditional kitchen construction and installation, stepping away from the concept of carcasses and multiple layers of composite and glued materials.

Unnecessary materials have been removed. Materials thicknesses have been reduced, such as drawer and door fronts, which are 8mm instead of the standard minimum of 16mm, and are also interchangeable. Doors and drawer fronts can even be reused from a previous kitchen. The traditional kitchen material types and applications have been completely revisited and switched to ones that don't contain and emit toxins, are recycled, can be separated and can be recycled – while still being durable. In fact, the user experience is improved through choices of coatings and counter tops that contain technology that purifies the air through a photocatalytic reaction, eliminating bacteria, viruses, fungi and bad smells.

By using an invisible induction hob under the porcelain counter, the hob's area can be used for cooking and food preparation – even chopping – so is multifunctional. It's also very easy to clean, with a reduced need for the use of cleaning products, again contributing to healthy indoor air quality.

Rosales' innovative design is primarily a mechanically fixed, self-supporting piece of modular storage, which can go on to be reused, updated functionally, repaired or the colour or finish changed. It's long lasting, so can be resold. It can even be adapted for other future uses, such as freestanding storage. It's certainly not something you'd want to leave behind when you move home!

FACTS

Founded: 2019

Founder: Paula Rosales

Visit: Showroom: 84 Zurbano Street, Madrid 28010, Spain www.kitchenforlife.es

explore

Graeme Brooker, *50/50 Words for Reuse – A Minifesto*, Canalside Press, 2022.

Duncan Baker-Brown, *The Re-Use Atlas: A Designer's Guide Towards the Circular Economy*, RIBA Publishing, 2024.

Bill Bensley, 'Sensible sustainable solutions', 2020, www.bensley.com/media/sensible-sustainable-solutions

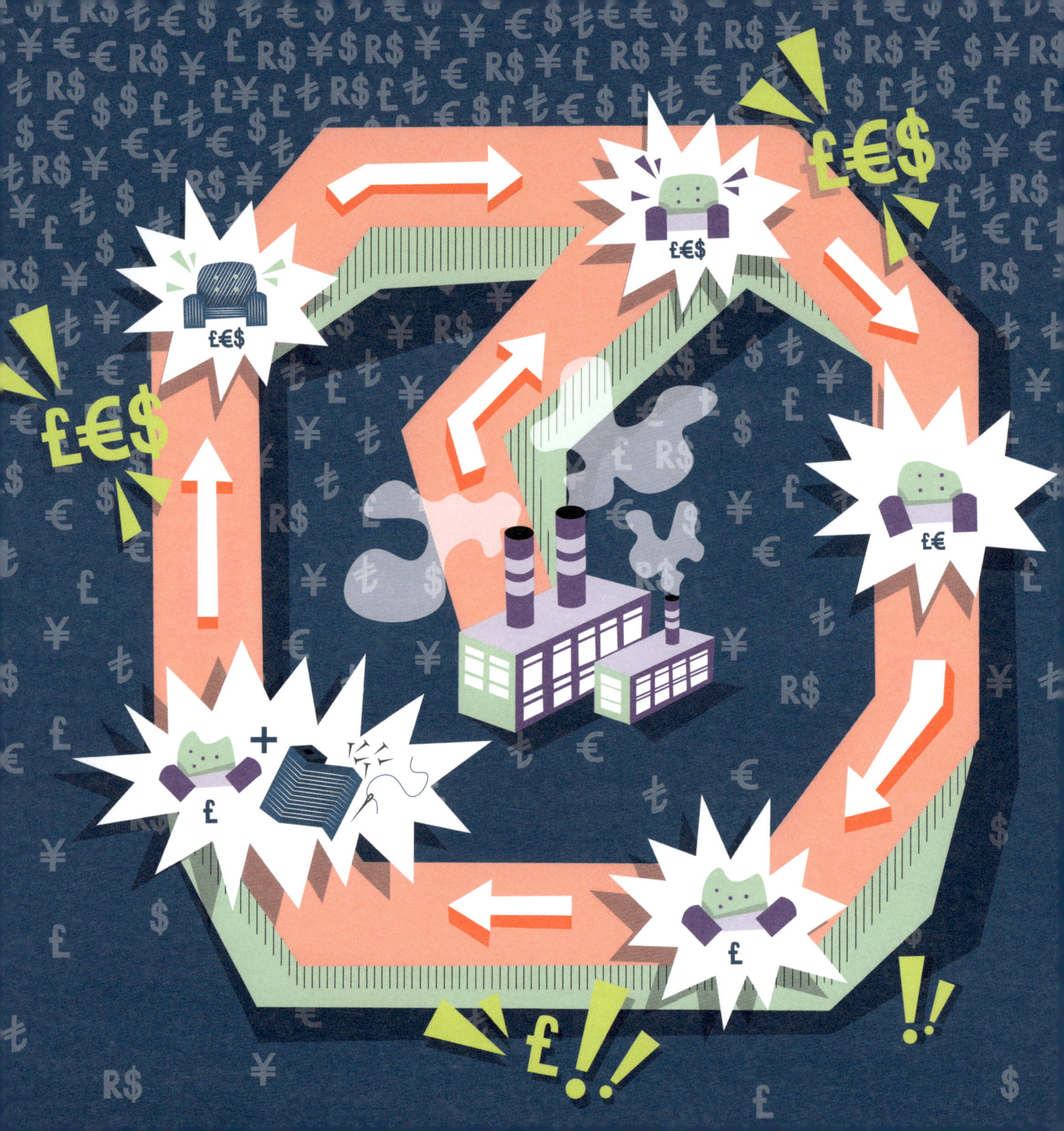

2

Circular Economy

Keeping materials at their most valuable for longest would be the easiest way to describe the circular economy. The 'economy' word seems to confuse people: in reality, the circular economy is a design system that *circulates*, where there is no concept of waste. The polluting and waste-creating cradle-to-grave model we have been so used to since the Industrial Revolution is a one-directional, irreversible and linear 'Take – Make – Waste'. It has one use, without thought for its impact from there on, or any potential further uses. The circular economy concept, in contrast, is of a constant loop where there is no 'away' to throw things. 'Waste is a resource in the wrong place,'[1] as resource expert Cat Fletcher (aka Resource Goddess) says.

There are finite resources, and designers are great problem-solvers. I find that an exciting combination. Switching to a process that is circular rather than linear provides the design industry with opportunities and possibilities. It's an efficient and business-savvy design method, and risk is reduced as the model is not connected to potentially volatile markets upstream in the early parts of the supply chain.

The Ellen MacArthur Foundation, the pioneering charity which is the world leader on education and encouragement of a circular economy, defines the circular economy as based on three principles, driven by design:

- Eliminate waste and pollution.

- Circulate products and materials (at their highest value).

- Regenerate nature.[2]

So, this means examining all processes and resources used (materials, energy, fossil fuels, water) and improving the systems used by business and citizens to sit within the remit of the resources we have, for the benefit of people and planet, nature and animals.

US architect William McDonough and German chemist Michael Braungart defined the concept of a cradle-to-cradle framework, inside which there are two cycles for materials to be 'eco-effective' within the circular economy.

- The first is the biological cycle, where the nutrients are designed to compost safely back into the soil without harm, and are regarded as food or nutrient.

- The second is the technical cycle: using metals and plastics that can continuously circulate, and that, through improved design, are durable, updateable and repairable; the concept is buying an output rather than owning a product.

At design stage, we need to create design that minimises waste through its lifespan: designs that can be disassembled and reassembled easily, that are loved or trusted, durable, repairable and easily upgradeable. For years we have been told to minimise damage. But being merely recyclable is not enough. Doing 'less harm' or being 'less bad' is not enough. Recycling as we have known it is now a last resort. Enhancing and upcycling should be the goal rather than causing any damage. The cradle-to-cradle framework encourages positive improvement through design. The framework is a methodology for the circular economy as well as being a certification process for products to be evaluated by.

According to William McDonough and Michael Braungart, 'The goal of the upcycle is a delightfully diverse, safe, healthy and just world with clean air, water, soil and power – economically, equitably, ecologically and elegantly enjoyed.'[3]

Designers are often already – without knowing it – working in a circular way, by reusing things from site, repairing or reviving things that the client already has, or sourcing unusual vintage finds. To really enhance your circular economy credentials, it's just about scaling up those principles and using them more consistently, with a better understanding of life cycles. It's also important to understand which 'cycle' materials sit within and how they loop back for future uses.

2.1 Meeting rooms were formed from reused windows, with a coffee counter made from salvaged old bank deposit boxes.

Circl

Amsterdam, Netherlands

Asking employees to donate 16,000 old pairs of jeans to use for insulation is not the usual way to engage stakeholders in a new building addition, but it was a clever one. The whole approach of this building's creation has been quite different.

On first appearance from outside, the Circl pavilion, built in the square alongside the head office of Dutch bank ABN AMRO, doesn't look all that large, blended with the garden beds that sit in front and dwarfed by the tall buildings around it in Amsterdam's Zuidas business district. It's actually a very spacious three floors, with a high-ceilinged basement added. This pioneering 'Living Lab' building – evolved to educate on the circular economy and commissioned by the bank – has been on a complicated but educational journey. The building, intended to be circular, demountable and reusable, is evidence of the perfect client, architect and project team collaborative combination.

It's clearly been a great learning process for the stakeholders. Each stakeholder in the creation of this building has seen a ripple effect in terms of lessons learned on this project being applied to other projects. It is testament to the client, who quickly recognised this building was not simply going to be another office building to fill with desks. The client was brave enough to pause the build and use it as an opportunity to show the ethos of their company and share learnings on the circular economy within it in a multitude of ways, both in-house and also to inspire the neighbourhood and the wider public using its bar, restaurant with kitchen garden, and the multifunctional spaces via exhibitions, debates, workshops, lectures, childcare, film screenings, markets and concerts.

I was surprised after seeing the Circl building, as its project lead architect Hans Hammink told me it was only the second sustainable project he'd worked on in his career. He explained the bank had been a long-standing client for his Amsterdam-based firm de Architekten Cie. Hammink had worked on many impressive

2.2 The restaurant area.

buildings globally for the bank, typically in the traditional materials of concrete, stone and marble. When he joined the project, the client had been exploring how the square in front of their headquarters could be better used. There was great potential for a building that could be used outside of office hours. The brief was very much evolving, various-sized meeting spaces were more and more needed. Other ventures were happening in the area, such as a new, improved-capacity railway station. The area was very built up and nature hadn't been a strong consideration. This new building was looking like it was on track to be another BREEAM 'excellent' certified building to match its neighbours, but the project team wanted to push the design more than that, seeking a more sustainable option. They asked: Could the heating and cooling be done in a better way? Could a greywater system be implemented for toilet flushing and watering the gardens? Hammink explained:

'As an architect, you're a service provider, which means you don't necessarily have everything in your control, but you do have the power to quiz the client and make them aware of the options. Your role is that of a catalyst, stimulating and enthusing your client. You can tell them a story that they identify with, that they support, and want to challenge. In that case, it can be useful if the client is and will remain the owner of the building as well, as the long-term perspective of a circular building will then be financially more interesting, as there will be more time to earn the investment back.'[4]

Hammink's approach was to apply the circular economy principles to produce an energy- and resource-efficient building, using many reused materials and designed to be disassembled and used again thanks to a thoughtful design and traceable material and product passport labels. Hammink avoided the typical 'off the shelf' construction approach and even the approach to ownership. For example, the building's lift and lighting are rented for their output rather than bought. As the bank owned the building, it was easy for them to see that this design approach had huge, longer-term benefits during the use stage: the embodied carbon (maintenance, repair, ease of replacement and refurbishment) and the operational carbon (reduced energy and water footprint through water-saving devices, which also has an energy-saving benefit). It's worth noting that by the time this ambitious redesign was presented to the client, the pavilion's concrete foundations were being constructed for the original design. The client took a leap of faith and supported the design. From here, the de Architekten Cie. project team collaborated with TU Delft (Hammink's alma mater) and the construction company BAM Amsterdam to swiftly redesign the building from this point on.

Meanwhile, the interior design team at Rotterdam-based interdisciplinary design studio DoepelStrijkers set to work on the interior design. DoepelStrijkers has much experience of working on circular economy projects, applying its in-house 'five material and object approaches' to its designs for the multifunctional spaces to minimise the use of virgin materials, ensuring ease of repair and design for disassembly:

1   Reuse 1:1

2   Reuse + remanufacture

3   Recycle

4   Reusable

5   Object as a service.

For future use as a reuse material bank, the team recorded all quantities and every element used to build, finish and furnish the building on an online materials passport.

2.3 The rooftop bar area.

2.4 The multifunctional ground-floor space.

2.5 The restaurant and bar have embraced circular principles throughout the menu. Fruit and vegetables are regularly preserved in jars and bottles to save waste, providing a colourful and ever-changing backlit display.

2.6 The basement meeting area, complete with reused furniture and rug on the sanded and sealed concrete floor.

2.7 Circl's restaurant.

Soon after the building was designed with this new approach, the Dutch government announced plans to make the Dutch economy fully circular by law by 2050.

The timber support structure is constructed from locally sourced larch, made a little over size so the fixing-hole sections could be cut off when dismantled and the beams reused as new. The beams are unpainted to make them easy to reuse. No bonding agents were used. Everything is dry fixed together using screws, bolts or clamps that can be undone.

The basement's main floor finish is simply the building's concrete base, which has been sanded and sealed. Instead of protecting the floors with disposable plastic covering during the build, scaffold towers for tradespeople to access ceilings and walls had special tyres added to prevent damage to the concrete.

Unnecessary additional materials were reduced, even removed, such as ceilings and concealing ducting. The basement concrete walls were left bare so no writing on walls by tradespeople during the build was allowed. Timber offcuts from the construction were saved and used as wall finishes.

The team at DoepelStrijkers designed clever moveable acoustic panels to make the ground floor easy to adapt for multiple uses – providing vertical divisions and also horizontal ones for dropping a ceiling, helping acoustic comfort or where intimacy is needed – all at the push of a button and made from recycled aluminium with acoustic dampening inside, using some of the denim collected from staff. An acoustic wall surface was created using recycled fibres from old uniforms collected from office staff.

The beautiful timber floors throughout the ground and first floor are made from rejected timber from a window-frame manufacturer and are a strong feature of the building.

Furniture has been urban-mined from the client's own spaces. Vintage furniture and salvaged items were used, including some exhibition display equipment from the Stedelijk Museum at 's-Hertogenbosch. Dirk van der Kooij chairs made from old refrigerators were installed. Some of the furniture is even for sale, with the space acting as a showroom for vintage furniture retailer

2.8 The multifunctional first and ground floor of Circl pavilion.

Mass Modern Design. The bank's own art collection has provided the artwork and sculptures on display.

DoepelStrijkers worked on the spatial concept alongside Ex Interiors for the restaurant and rooftop bar. The open kitchen even runs on a 100kW supply instead of the usual 200kW, which means lower-energy appliances and a creative approach to the menus so that high-energy-using fryers are not needed. The food supply deliveries are rationalised to reduce CO_2, which meant suppliers had to make positive changes within their own operations as a consequence. Seasonal and locally sourced ingredients take priority. The menu adjusts to suit what is available, rather than the other way round.

The gardens, external walls and landscaping on the roof and around the building have organic, native plants, added to encourage biodiversity, and Belgian cobblestones that had been used for a thousand years were reclaimed and reused. On the bar's roof are 260 locally made solar photovoltaic panels, with a further 260 panels fixed to the exterior walls, which provide direct current (DC) power to the building.

Horizontal and vertical geothermal heat exchangers heat and cool the building. Indoor climate is cleverly controlled by tiled floor areas using a combination of recycled concrete and phase-changing materials which change state to suit the temperature needs of the building, using minimal energy.

The ripples from this collaborative and inspiring project have been numerous and significant. Through it, the bank has challenged its industry, largely real estate, to follow its lead and address its methods. There is even encouragement to copy the design of the building. The learning experience has led to similar projects for de Architekten Cie. and the construction company. Hammink is consulting on circular economy led projects globally. The bank's staff have an enhanced working experience using the building and gardens. They are also experiencing the circular economy first-hand. Circularity has been applied to every element brought into the building. All stakeholders have examined their methodologies and learnt new ones which they have continued to work with. This industry-leading building slots neatly

2.9 On the second floor, the rooftop bar leads to the garden, providing calming places for staff and visitors to relax, with a solar-powered phone-charging station.

into the Amsterdam 'doughnut' model, which demonstrates how the city aims to provide the socio-economic measures necessary for the population to thrive, but all within our planetary boundaries, showcasing the city as one of the most sustainable cities in the world.

FACTS

Client: ABN AMRO bank

Interior design: DoepelStrijkers

Restaurant and rooftop bar design: Ex Interiors

Architect: de Architekten Cie.

Circularity adviser: TU Delft

Lighting designer: Beersnielsen

Completion: September 2017

Gross internal floor area: 3,350m^2

Visit: www.circl.nl

Circular Office

Düsseldorf, Germany

Urselmann Interior is a young design-and-build start-up, led by trained carpenter and project manager Sven Urselmann. He saw the 'design flaw' of waste in the interiors industry, how the reuse of materials was an afterthought and not part of the design brief at all, and wanted to be part of the solution to the problems of the waste-creating and resource-using construction industry. The feeling was that Urselmann Interior's own office, in Düsseldorf, had to be the test-bed and materials laboratory to experiment in and then demonstrate how to create a circular economy interior. After four years in business, the further decision was made to make it a co-working space so the lessons could be shared more widely with users.

Urselmann's discovery of the cradle-to-cradle circular economy theory was a lightbulb moment. This project gave the in-house team of designers and craftspeople the opportunity to collaboratively rethink how things are done and re-educate on materials and processes. There were two aspects to the experiment: the interior and its kitchen.

Designing, making and installing kitchen furniture had been a large part of the company's residential work. The design for the kitchen cabinetry was approached differently. Storage would no longer have a carcass, but instead a mechanically fixed timber frame, using the minimal thickness of materials needed. Timber was sourced from a very local poplar forest. A key area was to look at how to build a kitchen with standard modules and appliances, without fibre board or glue or waste. No coatings or finishes are added unless they are needed, to keep the material in the biological cycle so it will safely compost. Urselmann was concerned that standards may change over time and additives used now might be deemed unhealthy for tradespeople or the users in years to come, so only healthy materials that did not contain toxic chemicals were used. For doors, drawer fronts and shelves, the team experimented with 'Really', a wipeable, durable, 70% waste textile, solid-board material

2.10 Urselmann Interior's co-working office.

made by Kvadrat, with a closed-loop system where Kvadrat takes back the material at the end of use. The solution had to stand on an equal footing to the regular consumer offer, having an equal aesthetic, performance, lifespan and cost, and not purely aimed at a like-minded client. Most importantly, it needed to be repairable, reusable, dismantlable and safely compostable. Even though the cost of these more innovative materials while in lower production quantities is still pretty high, this kitchen design currently compares well to a bespoke, handmade, fully timber kitchen.

2.11 The kitchen design.

2.12 The main office of Urselmann Interior's co-working office.

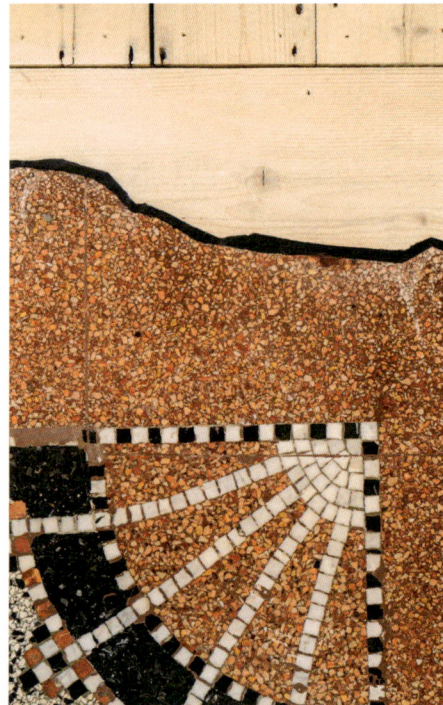

2.13 The beauty of where new and old floor meet. Some of the original mosaics.

Urselmann recognised that commercial clients, especially, enjoy the storytelling so are attracted to the products to set them apart from their competition. At the time I interviewed him, he was in discussion with the CEOs of two property developers to supply the kitchens in landmark circular economy buildings being built in Düsseldorf.

As the 74m^2 office interior – comprising a main office, meeting room and kitchen – was stripped out, the team quickly realised that removing the damaged ceiling and a layer of the floor alone was creating 4 tonnes of low-quality construction waste, which could only be landfilled or incinerated.

2.14 A minimal timber construction was added to the ceiling for cabling and acoustic panels, leaving the ceiling open.

The team wanted to create a new design language, one that steps away from glossy and perfect to appreciate imperfect finishes and patina, and to tell a story. An example is the floor, where some of the original mosaic terrazzo floor was retained and combined with newly fitted reclaimed timber flooring. This also saved any further site waste.

The business's supply chain was examined and the emphasis for specifications became the use of recycled, upcycled or biodegradable over virgin materials. Every component was listed in a published materials passport so it could be traceable in future. Where possible, it wanted to avoid virgin materials, so it partnered with urban-mining materials platform Concular to source reusable building materials such as meeting-room glass, lighting and radiators. Preloved LED office lamps were turned into lighting rafts, each with a recycled felt surround, which sit above the preloved desks in the main office. For anything new, Cradle to Cradle certification was used to select products. This third-party certification assesses the impact of manufactured products in five categories – material health, product circularity, clean air and climate protection, water and soil protection, and social fairness. The certification has five levels – platinum, gold, silver, bronze and basic – which are recertified every two years. Products used included Honext® (used as wall panelling, made from recycled paper and card), Giroflex seating and Merten System Design electrical sockets.

The office was decorated in Auro clay paint with a clay plaster ceiling, both finishes being breathable and able to help control humidity. Walls in the kitchen were made of a more durable lime plaster with wax finish.

Kitchen appliances were approached differently. The oven was preloved. The dishwasher was rented using Miele's rental model 'The UpGreat', where the company pays €24 euros a month to have clean dishes. The fridge was rented using Bosch's 'Blue Movement' subscription model. In both cases, maintenance and any repair are the responsibility of the appliance's manufacturer.

This new methodology came with challenges. Finishes that can't be mechanically fixed and need adhesives, such as tiles, needed extra research. The team partnered with both the Cradle to Cradle NGO and the C2C LAB building in Berlin, where they had experimented with clay to glue tiles in non-wet room areas. This enables the tiles to be later released and fully reused.

This positive, healthy and circular methodology is now Urselmann Interior's adopted way of working and is the result of collaboration, partnering, rethinking how things are done and the ability to experiment and share learning.

FACTS

Client, interior design, sustainability, acoustics, lighting: Urselmann Interior

Completion: April 2022

Gross internal floor area: 74m²

Visit: Lindenstraße 226, 40235 Düsseldorf, Germany, www.urslemann-interior.de

2.15 The Survivor Sofa.

2.16 Members of The Great Recovery team demonstrated the reupholstering process to visitors of Clerkenwell Design Week.

2.17 The Survivor Sofa project in progress at the 'Landfill to Festival'.

Survivor Sofa

UK, multiple locations

'The Survivor Sofa demonstrates the power of creativity and design in the rebirth of this sofa that was destined for landfill; it shines a light on the necessity of collaboration and communication in the service of a circular economy.'

Ella Doran, Designer in Residence, The Great Recovery, and Director of Ella Doran Design [5]

I learnt about this eye-opening project through my circular economy group, Circular Brighton & Hove, where we watched the documentary made by filmmaker Paul Hyatt which had also aired on UK television and headlined at the Crafts Council Reel to Real Film Festival in 2016. Circular Brighton & Hove is an enthusiastic, collective mix of mostly small businesses, championing zero waste via food, drink, fashion, textiles, renewable energy, electronics, the built environment, school uniform and baby clothes. There are more than 270 of these clubs globally, and I really recommend you seek one out and join a similar circular economy group. I've found it enjoyable and educational being involved in mine.

The UK's Waste and Resources Action Programme (WRAP) wanted to understand what bulky waste types were being collected kerbside and at recycling centres across the UK. In 2012, the charity undertook research recording and analysing what was collected and taken, and found that furniture made up around 42% of bulky waste (670,000 tonnes per year) and over 20% of it was instantly reusable and a further 25% was reusable with a slight repair.[6] The Survivor Sofa evolved from these findings as one of the projects by The Great Recovery, a subsequent initiative to examine and rethink how things are designed and made to prevent this waste.

Tasked with asking the question, 'How can we design better systems that will increase rates of reuse and reduce the quantity of bulky items reaching landfill and incineration?', the cross-industry changemaker charity Royal Society for Arts, Manufactures and Commerce (RSA) partnered with recycling and waste company SUEZ to create The Great Recovery. Led by The Great Recovery's founder Sophie Thomas, a team of the RSA's Designers in Residence embarked on a ten-day investigation of the current system and was tasked with making recommendations for closing the loop on furniture waste.

The group visited a waste transfer station and community recycling centre in Leatherhead as a typical sample, to see what was happening with consumer 'waste'. The multiskilled team was made up of textile and surface designer Ella Doran, business and service expert Sarah Johnson, technical designer Kirsty Ewing and designer/maker Xenia Moseley. They talked to the people working at the centre to exchange insights and look at what was being dropped off by the public. They pulled a two-year-old sofa from a skip in great condition, but it didn't have the all-important fire-safety label attached which would give it the passport to a further life. Globally, according to UN-Habitat, 99% of the things we buy are disposed of within six months.[7] After talking to Adrian Collins of Kingston Community Furniture, who collects and resells furniture, the team discovered that only about half of the sofas donated could be resold for this reason. Fire-safety labels are often in a prominent place that irritates users and flap about so people tear them off without knowing the future consequences of removal.

Xenia Moseley explained:

'Studying product design and going to the Milan Furniture Fair... you see how much stuff is being made and, as a designer, you are encouraged to contribute to that. The circular economy needs to be taught as an essential part of design education as we come to understand that many of the resources we rely on are finite. As backwards as it may seem, when creating a product, designers must ask themselves, 'What kind of waste do we want it to be?'[8]

The team collaborated with Urban Upholstery, who are designer, architect and artist Patrizia Sottile and established upholsterer Andrea Simonutti. They specialise in giving contemporary new life to great-quality old furniture, often rescued after being abandoned on streets. Councils often won't collect if there's no fire-safety label. Sottile and Simonutti turn the furniture into pieces of art, heirlooms that people love. They showed The Great Recovery team a beautiful Chesterfield sofa they'd brought back to life. They completely reapproached the original design, leaving much of the frame exposed with loose cushions sitting on top.

Together with The Great Recovery team, they stripped down to the frame the two-year-old sofa that had been salvaged from the skip (which they named Survivor Sofa) and timed the process. Due to its well-made build quality, the exercise took the six of them 3 hours 24 minutes. It had been robustly made with lots of staples, plastic webbing and board attached to the beech frame. They then took apart an abandoned £200 mass-market chaise longue. This simpler assembly just took 44 minutes to strip to the frame, due to fewer staples and the fact it was made from cheaper materials. Frustratingly, the fire-safety label was found under the top fabric on the lining so it could have been reused. This just reaffirmed that fire-safety labels need to have a consistent common position or be made permanent so they can't be removed at all. The team also concluded from the process that there needs to be a way to easily retest for fire safety to keep furniture in use. They also realised that a deconstruction manual, the reverse of an assembly manual, would be of huge benefit at the furniture's eventual end of life.

The team worked with Camira Fabrics to develop an innovative fabric made from 30% recycled textile fibre. Combined with a 100% recycled textile waste as filling, the Survivor Sofa was reupholstered, leaving parts of the frame on show as a new aesthetic in an interactive workshop event 'Landfill to Festival' for The Great Recovery at Clerkenwell Design Week in 2015.

The project team's findings and analysis resulted in recommendations that were shared with the furniture-making industry, and also with waste managers, policymakers and local authorities – along with 'Future Scenarios for Furniture' key recommendations to close the loop on bulky waste:

1   Fire-safety labels: should be a permanent but unobtrusive attachment.

2   Alternative futures and deconstruction manual: a guide to useful disposal should encourage reuse, takeback, repair and resale.

3   Design for contract, rent and remanufacture: quality design for effective remanufacturing, storage and redistribution.

4   'Own Art' design services: finance models should be developed to make access to long-lasting quality affordable.

5   Entrepreneurial logistics: use social media to create formalised reuse zones to avoid fly-tipping and waste through weather damage and careless handling.

6   Ingredients tags and provenance tracking: QR codes and innovative labelling should be used to track materials.

7   Recertification pack: develop a 'branding' device to fire-safety test and permanently label recertified items on the spot, without needing to be transported to a test centre.[9]

Sophie Thomas, Project Director of The Great Recovery, said:

'We don't have a limitless supply of materials coming in and out of our systems. This sofa represents all the abandoned but still usable products which are discarded for being 'off trend'. These products assemble on street corners wishing for a second home but are abandoned with no other choice than heading along the straight-to-landfill pathway of resource doom. We've redirected the power of design towards the rebirth of our Survivor Sofa.'[10]

2.18 The Survivor Sofa now permanently resides in the reception of RSA House, London.

FACTS

Client: The Great Recovery – a project which ran between 2012 and 2016, instigated by the **RSA,** working with funding and support from **Innovate UK**

RSA Designers in Residence: Ella Doran, Kirsty Ewing, Sarah Johnson, Xenia Moseley with Patrizia Sottile and Andrea Simonutti, Urban Upholstery

RSA project team: Sophie Thomas, Lucy Chamberlain, Josie Warden

Wider team: The Great Recovery's network, Surrey County Council, SUEZ, Global Action Plan, Camira Fabrics, London Reuse Network and Surrey Reuse Network

Completion: 2015

Visit: RSA House, 8 John Adam Street, London, WC2N 6EZ, UK

Q explore

de Architekten Cie., *Lessons in Circularity*, 2021, www.cie.nl/ebook-circularity?lang=en

Ellen MacArthur Foundation, website, videos and podcast, www.ellenmacarthurfoundation.org

Circular economy clubs: www.circulareconomyclub.com

Cradle to Cradle certified products registry: www.c2ccertified.org/products/registry

William McDonough and Michael Braungart, *Cradle to Cradle: Remaking the Way We Make Things*, North Point Press, 2002

William McDonough and Michael Braungart, *The Upcycle: Beyond Sustainability – Designing for Abundance*, North Point Press, 2013

TU Delft, online course: Delftx CircularXCircular Economy:

An Introduction, www.edx.org/learn/circular-economy/delft-university-of-technology-circular-economy-an-introduction

Ken Webster, 'Circular economy', TEDxLoodusele talk, Loodusele, October 2011, www.youtu.be/mvQEBB3IdZM?si=5L6iGHAJOA_V7DhJ

Paul Wyatt, 'The Survivor Sofa Story' (documentary), 2015, www.paulwyatt.co.uk/the-survivor-sofa-story-now-online

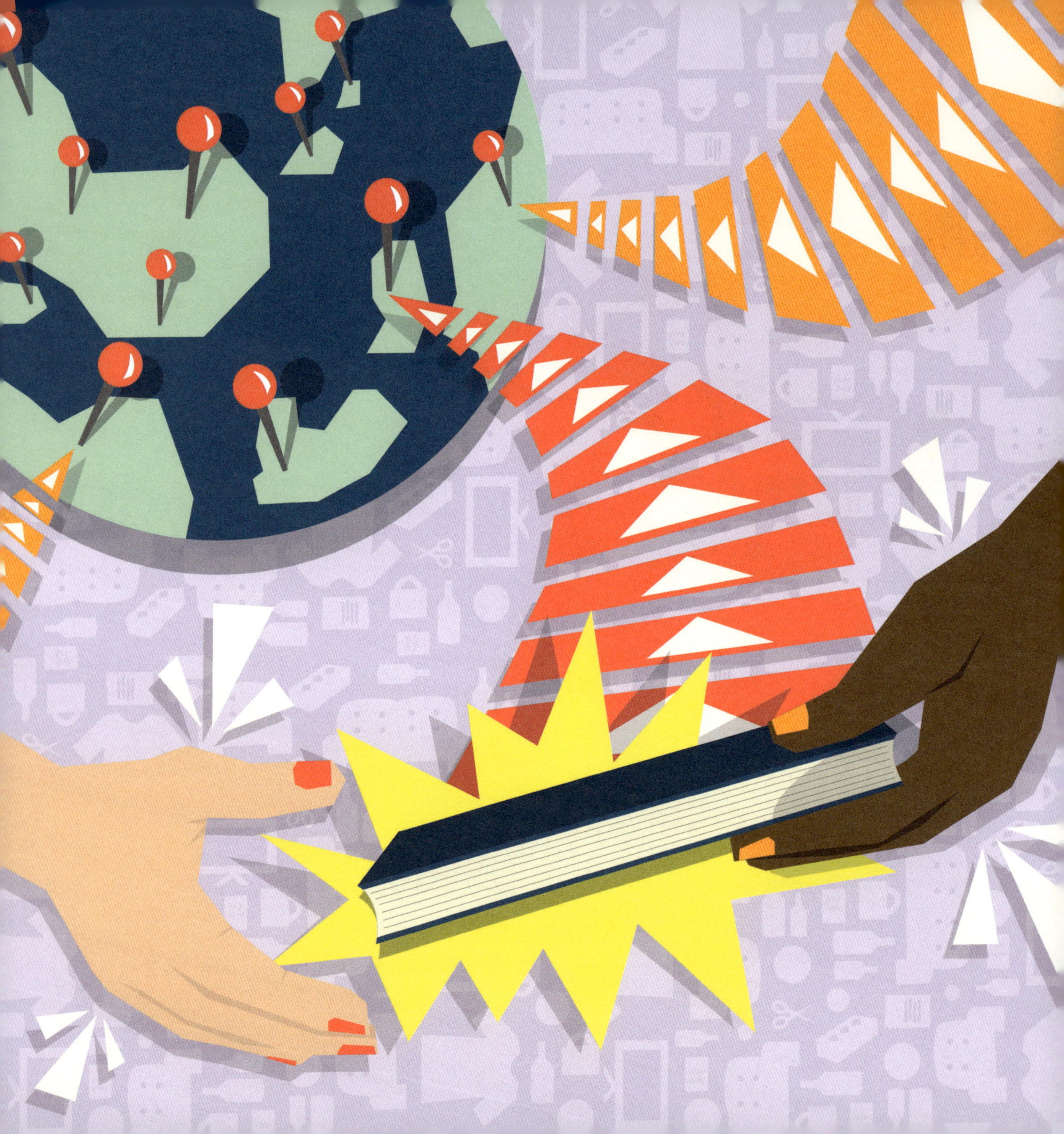

3

Sharing Economy

❛ The sharing economy is a system to live by where we care for people and planet and share available resources in any way that we can. Action, creativity and collaboration are our way out of this climate crisis. We have the solutions. We need to use our resources positively. ❜

Benita Matofska, international speaker and consultant on sustainability and the sharing economy and author of Generation Share – The Change-Makers Building the Sharing Economy[1]

In pursuit of the definition of the sharing economy, I interviewed Benita Matofska. Her book documenting the stories of changemakers worldwide creating sharing-economy initiatives was made with photographer and visual storyteller Sophie Sheinwald. Together they defined the sharing economy in a multitude of ways through 200 interviews with those who make, repair, improve, rescue, crowdfund and finance – by sharing skills, food, resources, pets, toys, human breast milk, transport, tents, workspaces and homes.

Matofska identified what has caused the rise in the sharing of resources, notably since the Covid-19 pandemic. The rise is rooted in efficient use of resources and in community, offering opportunity and a fresh approach to how buildings and interior spaces are created using resources more responsibly. These fresh approaches include:

- digital nomad culture – how home and work is transient and fluid; the detachment from 'stuff'

- rethinking of the office – including co-working of individuals or businesses within shared spaces and the influences and community that come from that

- co-living driven by the increased cost of living and the need for social contact

- better-connected communities and cross-generational living

- maker, hacker and repair culture – networking people, skills and resources, forming communities and continuing skills and crafts.

So why are we fixated on ownership and 'stuff'?

Over the past 100 years in particular, humanity – particularly in developed economies – has gone from relative scarcity to an abundance of 'stuff'. Trend forecaster and cultural commentator James Wallman writes about this in his book *Stuffocation – Living More with Less*,[2] highlighting how we have gone from frugal and careful consumers to conspicuous consumerism which comes complete with the stress around that ownership. He writes about research on the negative impact of clutter on our health,[3] why we hold on to it and the benefits of letting go. Wallman encourages us to recognise this and focus on experiences instead. He writes about the experiment that podcasters and writers Joshua Fields Millburn and Ryan Nicodemus – known as 'The Minimalists' – carried out on their lives; to live with less. The resulting happiness changed their view of ownership: 'Not buying something is letting it go in advance.'[4] Through their '16 rules for living with less', Millburn and Nicodemus promote the joy of sharing experiences with other people that will enhance your life overall.

We no longer regard possessions with the respect we once did. Heirlooms are rare. We would once hand down the generations all kinds of property, such as jewellery, furniture and antiques – as we might still do now – but also bedlinen, clothes and other things that still had a life and usefulness. Why do we have this fascination with the new over quality and longevity? Why are we not linking this pursuit of happiness and status through materialism to its social and environmental impact? Marie Kondo's KonMari Method™ is her process to select and reduce possessions based on whether objects 'spark joy' or not. Jonathan Chapman calls the resilience of this relationship between consumers and products 'emotional durability'.[5] Thoughtfully collected and gathered items bring with them memories and happiness, and that connection generally comes with an extended lifespan.

In his book *The Circular Economy: A User's Guide*,[6] architect Walter Stahel suggests a focus on what we experience from a product rather than our ownership of it. The sharing economy – a concept focused on experience or output, rather than actual ownership

– works so well for interiors: paying for the benefit for the time something is used and needed (object as a service) rather than paying for the object itself. Why does everything in a space need to be owned? Possessions come with a burden of ownership, of maintaining, repairing and being responsible for passing on, recycling, disposal. How long something is needed for can vary greatly and shouldn't mean quality is reduced if it is only needed for a shorter period. This is sadly where 'fast' furniture comes in to fill that gap – and just like fast fashion, it has a short life and horrible repercussions for the environment and workers within the supply chain. The sharing economy provides a huge opportunity for an improved approach.

Multifunctional spaces or multifunctional objects ensure a maximised, extended use. Furniture, for example, may need to adapt to the needs of the user and grow with them, like a cleverly designed bed that adapts to suit a growing child or an item that can be designed to be multipurpose, therefore increasing its usefulness. We need to make spaces as useful and busy to maximise their material to use ratio.

The sharing economy feels like an exciting way to fill and revive vacant shops and banks with places to repair and share from. The Library of Things, a lending library of home and garden equipment and tools, is already doing this successfully in multiple locations in the UK.

3.1 View into a dining area, showing ZZ Driggs furniture.

ZZ Driggs

Brooklyn, USA

After observing unethical supply chains, waste and planned obsolescence within the furniture industry, ZZ Driggs founder Whitney Frances Falk could see an opportunity in combining high-quality and beautifully made furniture made by independent designers with the sharing economy. Falk evolved from a career in finance to commissioning contemporary furniture and collecting fine furniture. Both are showcased for rent, for sale (or both) from her platform, making high-quality design and skilful workmanship more widely accessible.

In directly opposing the notion of trends and fast furniture, this alternative ownership concept attracted likeminded investors to her business as funding rounds happened. The business is now multi-award-winning and B Corp certified, demonstrating an alternative way to furnish homes and businesses while doing business ethically and being an attractive employer. Over a third of products available have an independent third-party certification, all are built to last at least 50 years and all suppliers use locally sourced materials. ZZ Driggs' designers and makers are celebrated on the website, with the company pledging to commit a minimum of 15% of annual purchasing to black-owned businesses to lead and rebalance.

Attracting customers has been approached differently as well. ZZ Driggs has commissioned BAFTA-winning director Stefan Hunt to produce a short film. Day-trip itineraries are devised for design-history visits, such as to the former home of industrial designer Russel Wright. The company has raised awareness around the impacts of toxic chemical use in the interior design industry by publishing its 'ZZ's List of Future Banned Items' and also fast-furniture life-cycle analysis.

3.2 A ZZ Driggs sideboard in a living area.

FACTS

Founded: 2014

Founder and CEO: Whitney Frances Falk

Awards: Winner of Fast Company's Innovation by Design Award, three-time Webby winner, Anthem Award winner for Social Impact/Most Sustainable Business Model, Dezeen's Website of the Year

Certification: Certified B Corporation™

Visit: www.zzdriggs.com

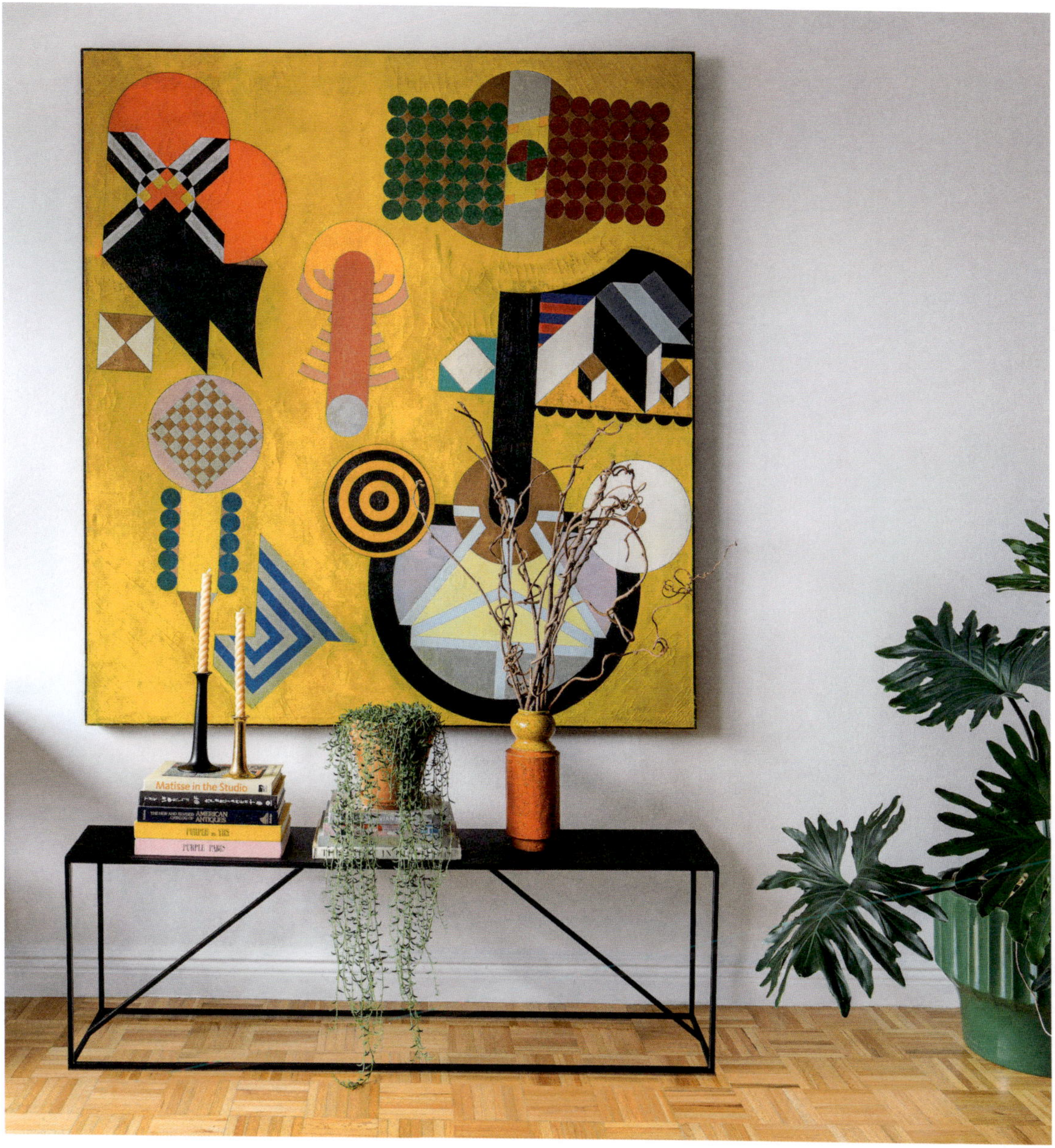

3.3 A ZZ Driggs coffee table.

3.4 Mozilla Factory Space office. Pallets were reworked to make modular raised flooring sections with cable management and floor box access panels.

Mozilla Factory Space headquarters

Tokyo, Japan

Technology plays a vital role for good in this connection of community within the sharing economy; from highly efficient ways of sharing skills, spaces and resources to sharing knowledge of how a building and elements within it are made.

Post-pandemic, we are rethinking how offices are used so that real estate is optimised efficiently, saving money and carbon emissions as well as enhancing the experience for those using them, making them attractive to be in. There are designers using the sharing economy to share the actual designs that created the interiors. Open source is used widely for free-to-access software and the open-source movement encourages collaborative use of the software in order to help its improvement. How fitting for the world's largest open-source software community – Mozilla Japan, part of the Mozilla Foundation – to take that a step further and have open-source furniture designed for their Japanese headquarters in a former factory. The creators of the Firefox web browser engaged the team at NOSINGER, who creatively designed to their brief – an adaptable, quick-to-build, low-cost and functional event and workspace, with all drawings freely available online for everyone to access and replicate.

Found regular objects (like crates and pallets) and regular sheet products (like polycarbonate sheets and pine planks) were combined with a folded metal corner component to make dividers, shelves, counters, desks and even a pendant light. Crates were reused and hacked to make self-watering planters. To complete the software theme, the concept even has its own pixelated typeface used for wayfinding signage, WC signs and mirrors.

All drawings are downloadable from the OS Furnitures site. This multi-award-winning concept has now been replicated many times globally.

3.5 Adaptable panels – white boards or room dividers.

FACTS

Client: Mozilla Japan

Interior design: Eisuke Tachikawa, Kunihiko Sato (NOSINGER)
Graphic Design: Toshiyuki Nakaie (NOSINGER)

Completion: 2013

Gross internal floor area: unknown

Visit: www.os-furnitures.tumblr.com/post/53745111811/whats-open-source-furniture

3.6a,b,c   The open-source drawings show how to make the corner module component, which can be used in multiple ways.

WikiHouse + Opendesk

London, UK

Conscious of the huge consumption of materials and creation of waste in the building industry and the inequity of access to the built environment, the designers behind WikiHouse, Alastair Parvin, Nick Ierodiaconou and their collaborators, wanted to create a new system to help move the industry towards more sustainable ways of building, introducing efficiencies and bio-based materials.

Developed within their design studio Architecture 00, the WikiHouse concept takes open source one step further by sharing building blueprints as programming code for digital fabrication. Using readily available Forestry Stewardship Council (FSC®) certified sheet material and a 4ft by 8ft CNC (computer numerical control) cutting machine (a machine often used by DIYers and small industry globally), the code produces CNC-machined pieces. These pieces are simply fixed together using wedge-and-peg connections to build a house. The mallet can even be cut from the blueprint. Every piece is designed to be safely lifted and the joint connections are designed to be essentially mistake-proof.

WikiHouse is democratising the production and distribution of high-quality architecture with the aim to make it as accessible as possible to regular citizens. Rather than simply sharing a blueprint for a building, WikiHouse shares the full 'recipe' to making a building, which both speeds up the process and makes it a community-led endeavour through sharing the research and development, while decentralising the manufacturing by using independent local workshops to manufacture the parts using standard and widely available materials and processes.

Founded by WikiHouse cofounder Nick Ierodiaconou along with architect and furniture designer Joni Steiner, Opendesk originated from a commission by London-based digital start-up Mint Digital. Mint approached Architecture 00 to design its workspace, including commissioning furniture for it, which encouraged Ierodiaconou and Steiner to rethink the office design model. They created designs that followed the CNC-cut kit of parts principle of WikiHouse. The benefit of this was especially valued later, when Mint Digital was opening its New York office – the designs were simply sent to a local fabricator in Brooklyn to make locally rather than shipping the heavy assembled furniture all that way. Through this experiment, Opendesk was conceived. CNC had proved to be a robust and established technology that was easily shareable and cost effective globally.

With the goal of changing the furniture supply chain by linking customers to local makers globally, and therefore creating an ethical supply chain, Opendesk connects its designs to customers via a global network of local makers with their own workshops. Quotes are gathered by Opendesk and sent to the customers to choose from, depending on cost, reviews and timings. Waste is minimised as the designs are made on demand, and the components are efficiently designed to be cut from furniture-grade FSC® certified Baltic birch plywood and finished in a clear matt natural hard wax oil. The local maker then delivers the items as a flatpack kit and assembles the pieces on site, in the agreed lead time. There's no unnecessary bulky storage or expensive shipping required.

Opendesk's distributed manufacturing concept has been used for many workspaces, including Greenpeace, Google and WeWork. There are furniture designs available for use in education and homes as well.

Opendesk is working to widen the model to include other sheet materials that are available utilising local waste materials, such as solid timber. These include Smile Plastics, who form marbleised sheets from recycled yoghurt pots and other post-consumer waste plastic. Solid Wool is a sheet material made from bio-resin and waste wool. Foresso uses waste timber that is chipped and mixed with a sawdust and bio-resin binder to create a timber terrazzo. Kvadrat 'Really' fibre board is made from recycled textiles. Opendesk envisages a future where physical products are made locally, by locally owned independent manufacturers, keeping the benefits in the local economy, and making cities into producers.

3.7 A WikiHouse meeting room at Hub Westminster, a joint venture between The Hub Network, Architecture 00 and Westminster Council, which was a co-working and event space for impact-driven businesses. Although this meeting room no longer exists in this location, the hub network still exists.

3.8 The 'lift standing desk'.

This is a move towards the 'Fab City' model that grew from forward-thinking urbanists in Barcelona. These products would be increasingly made from locally sourced and, crucially, non-extractive materials, 'geofencing' to limit product and material choice to what is sensibly available locally and, in doing so, turning the 20th-century manufacturing model on its head.

One example from the range of furniture designs available is the 'lift standing desk', an adjustable-height sit/stand workbench, designed and shared by the cofounders of Opendesk. The design can be configured to varying dimensions, anything from a single desk up to a back-to-back bank of six or eight desks, and has been downloaded around 14,000 times globally for local on-demand manufacture.

FACTS

WIKIHOUSE

Founded: 2011

Founders: Architecture 00: Alastair Parvin, Nick Ierodiaconou

Award: TED City 2.0 prize, 2012

Visit: www.wikihouse.cc

OPENDESK

Founded: 2013

Founders: Joni Steiner and Nick Ierodiaconou, with Ian Bennink, Tim Carrigan and James Arthur

Downloads: 14,000

Visit: www.opendesk.cc

3.9 The Bide – a two-person, tiny-house holiday cabin.

The Bide

Milton Abbas, UK

What do you get when you combine a furniture buyer, an architect, a CNC machine and a plot on the side of a working farm?

You get The Bide, a beautiful holiday cabin. It scores more sharing-economy points as it's also created from a WikiHouse structure design, and the concept was from a knowledge-sharing exhibition visited by its owners.

The inspiration for the luxurious but tiny dwelling came from visiting Berlin's Bauhaus Archive Museum, where a tiny-house university – 'TinyU' – was set up in the courtyard of the museum's campus for its centenary in 2017–18, in conjunction with a group of architects whose self-built tiny houses were displayed and toured by visitors. The concept for the year-long knowledge-sharing event, called 'Tiny Houses Meet Global Challenges',[7] had come from the fact the courtyard was a conservation area so nothing permanent could be built. The concept of dwellings built on a trailer instead – which did not need planning permission – went on to be the concept for the exhibition, which was an opportunity to share the benefits for housing, shelter for refugees, workshops, co-working and other third spaces where ideas can be exchanged.

Caroline Jenkinson and Scott Lewis, the owners of The Bide, set themselves a tight brief. They wanted to create a holiday rental cabin that would be comfortable and attractive for year-round rental appeal, large enough to comfortably accommodate a super-king-sized bed (made from recycled denim) but also small enough fit on a 6.6m by 2.5m flatbed trailer to be taken across the UK to the site in Dorset. The ecological footprint was extremely important; not only did the structure need to sit literally lightly on the land, but it had to have a light impact on the planet as well. It was important to minimise the embodied energy of materials used in the structure and minimise the operational carbon used. The cabin was built to Passive House principles of low energy use through super insulation, robust airtight construction with a decentralised mechanical

3.10 The large bed is on the mezzanine above the bathroom and recessed kitchenette area and a curated library is displayed on the recessed, double-height bookcase alongside it in the main area. A projector screen can be stretched across the area for use with the projector for movie nights.

ventilation heat recovery (MVHR) system and triple glazing. There are water-saving measures installed in the form of a waterless toilet and a water-saving vapourised shower to lessen the ecological footprint.

Jenkinson and Lewis explained, 'Wikihouse was very enabling, giving us the agency to create something beautiful and bespoke without the price tag that would be associated with a master craftsman.'[8]

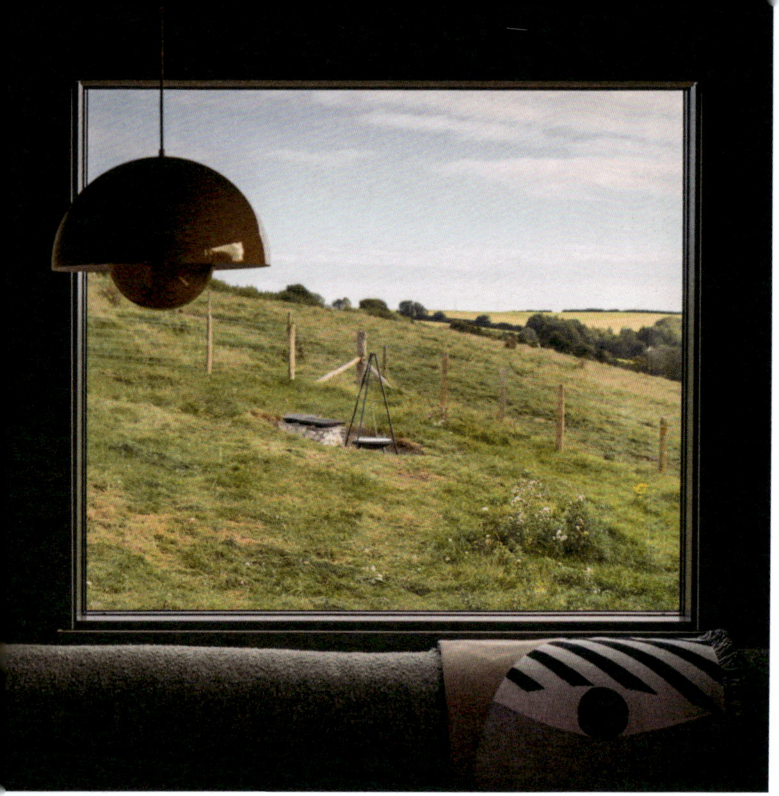
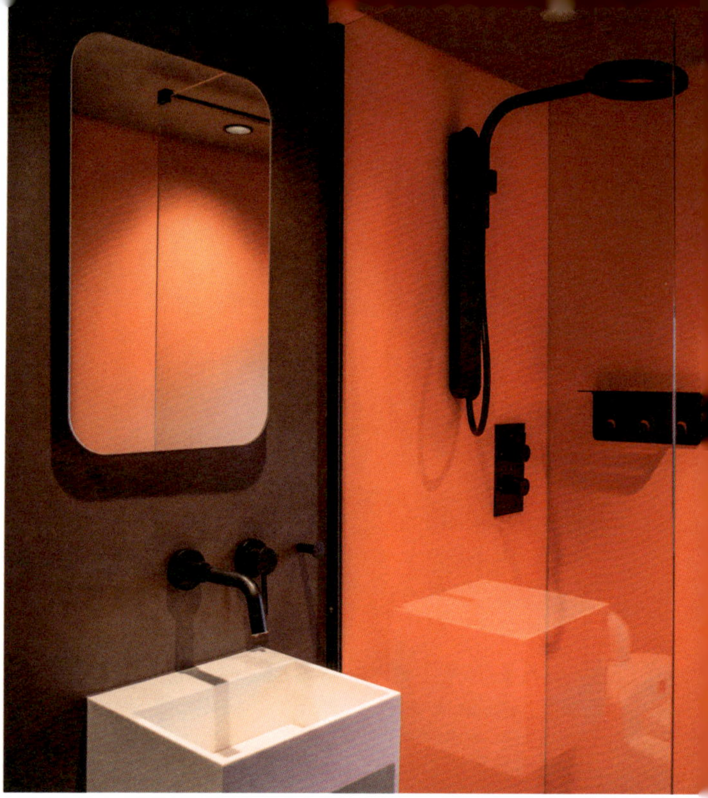
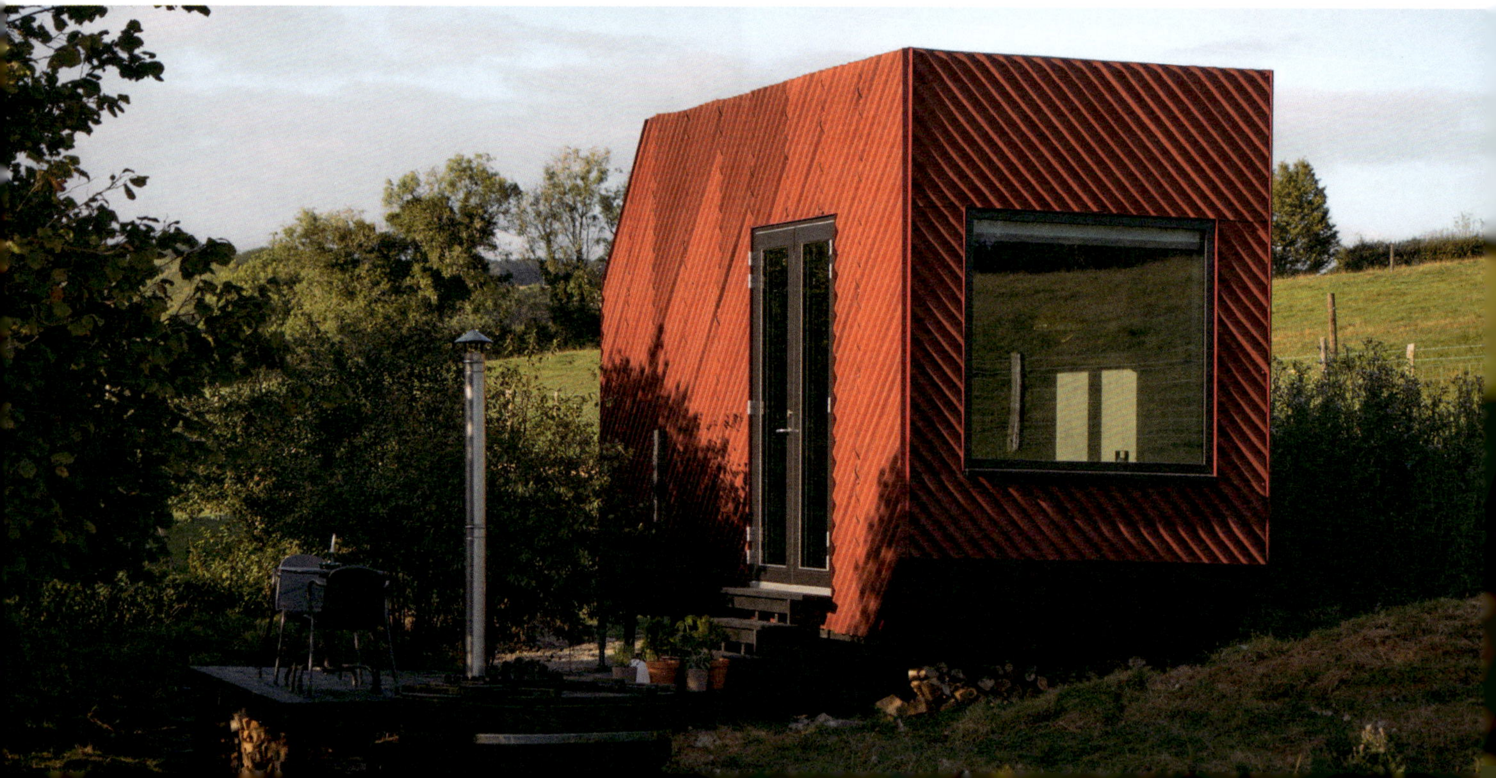

Inspired by the clever solutions on display in Berlin, the couple began to plot out their own version. Using a WikiHouse system was attractive as it gave Jenkinson and Lewis the opportunity to be self-builders by assembling the structure quickly, at lower cost and without requiring any carpentry skills. However, their furnishing and architecture skills are very clearly evident in how the cabin was designed and specified around the WikiHouse structure, which was adapted for insulation and waterproofing; internally, bespoke recessed furniture and clever storage solutions were used to maximise the spaciousness of the interior and make their own creative stamp on it. Their concept is contemporary and bold, with a colour scheme inspired by Swedish colourist Tekla Evelina Severin. Even the exterior manages to be contrasting yet also in keeping with its rural surroundings, as the rust-crimson-red cladding stands out from the surroundings yet is reminiscent of regular agricultural cladding. Simply by using the cladding on the diagonal, it instantly looks modern and unlike any rural cabin you might expect to find.

Robust but luxurious wood fibre panels coloured with organic dyes are used to line the interior walls and ceilings, with linoleum floors. The matte textures and fabrics layer and contrast with the high-gloss Verner Panton feature pendant light.

Costing just £40,000 and eight months of their own labour, the cabin has been loved by visitors, with some even thinking of doing similar projects themselves. Spurred on by their farmer landlord, the couple are working on a treehouse holiday home to accompany this stylish little cabin.

3.11 The main area is designed around a central picture window with restorative views to the farm and hills beyond.

3.13 Outside is a deck made from scaffold planks stained black, with a fire pit, seating area and a sunken wood-fired hot tub, screened by the coppice alongside.

3.12 The bathroom, complete with waterless toilet and water-saving vapourised shower.

FACTS

Client: Caroline Jenkinson, Scott Lewis

Interior design: Caroline Jenkinson, Scott Lewis

Architect: WikiHouse and Lewis & Mallon Architects

Frame CNC services: Quad CNC

Completion: 2021

Gross internal floor area: 18m²

Visit: The Bide, Milton Abbas, Dorset, www.thebide.com

explore

Joshua Fields Millburn and Ryan Nicodemus, 'The Minimalists' podcast, https://www.theminimalists.com

Benita Matofska and Sophie Sheinwald, *Generation Share – The Change-Makers Building the Sharing Economy*, Policy Press, 2019.

ZZ Driggs, 'ZZ's List of Future Banned Items', https://zzdriggs.com/blogs/research/zz-s-list-of-future-banned-items-and-their-conscious-counterparts

Mozilla Factory Space open-source furniture download: https://os-furnitures.tumblr.com/post/53745111811/whats-open-source-furniture

Alastair Parvin, 'Architecture for the people by the people', TED 2013: The Young. The Wise. The Undiscovered, Long Beach, May 2013.

James Wallman, '"Stuffocation" and the Experience Revolution', TEDxLSE, 3 May 2016.

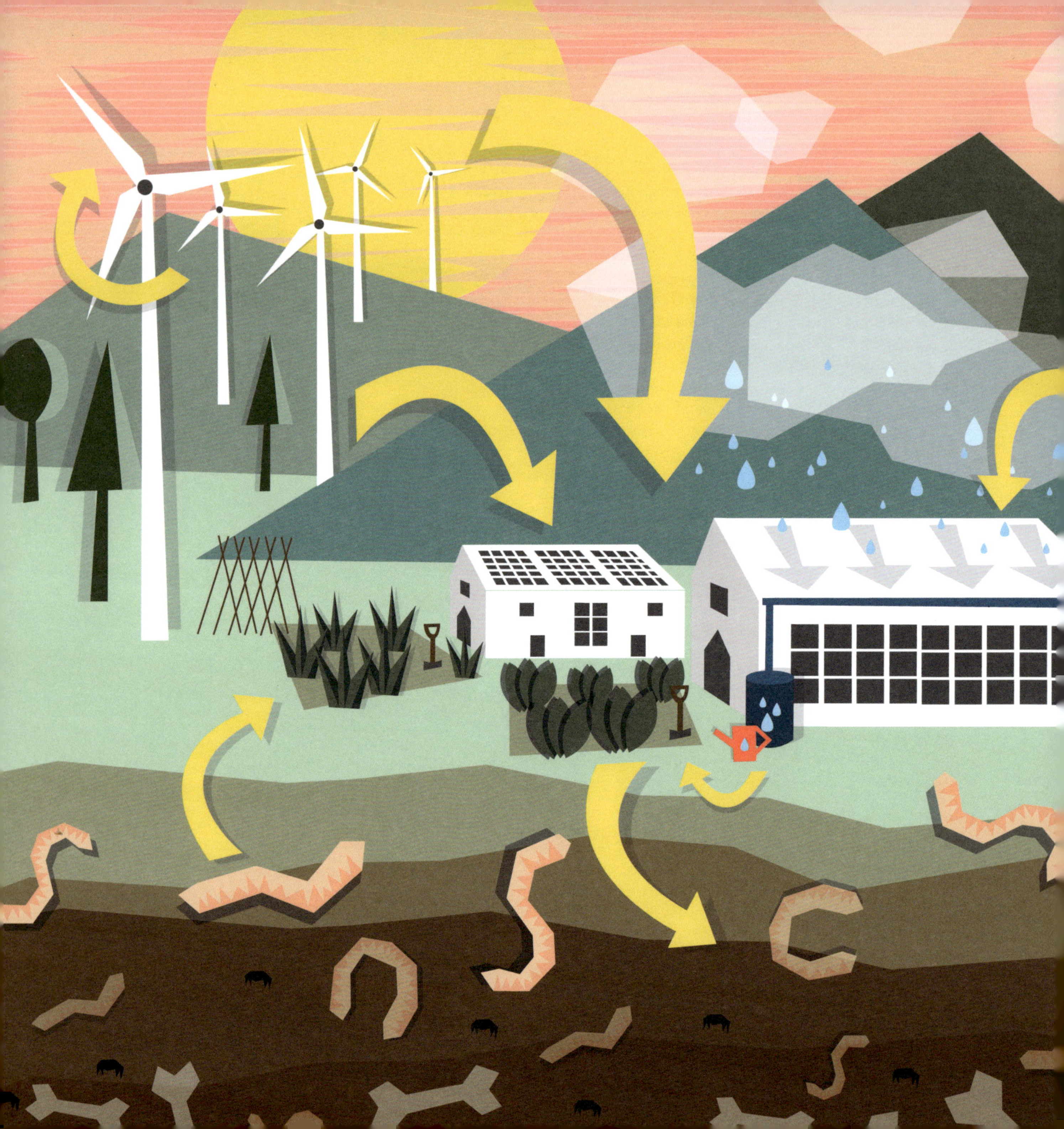

4

Regenerative Design

Regenerative design really needs to be where we are working now. Using materials and methods that are 'less bad' or simply 'sustainable' is no longer enough. We are not reducing our impact quickly enough and as designers we should be looking to go further and 'regenerate' through our selections and designs. Interior designers are increasing their awareness of the repercussions of the materials we use and understanding what is in them.

We need to recognise our interdependence with nature, and work with its systems and not exploit them, by rethinking the impact of our work through the whole lifespan so there is no harm at any point. In addition to lessening the harm of our footprint, we need to have a net-positive 'handprint' by supporting nature and the environment, by replenishing and enhancing it through our specifications and designs, working regeneratively rather than sustainably.

Not all seemingly 'natural' materials are regenerative. Regenerative materials must be safely compostable at the end of their life, so should not have chemical-intensive processes to create them, such as chemical additives. Some chemical additives are not so obvious: for example, chemical additives are sometimes added to crops used to supplement feed for grazing sheep, whose wool is later used for materials by our industry, making it non-regenerative. [1] These non-regenerative processes make it difficult for such materials to safely rot down at the end of life, and they therefore have the potential to pollute nature's essential all-life-supporting soil, air or waterways.

Regeneration is not only about material choices. Regenerative design is also about the built environment our projects sit within and the opportunity to ensure that the impact of those spaces is net-positive on the surrounding ecology and communities. This can be done by incorporating urban agriculture and green spaces planted with native species, using clean energy and energy efficiencies, sequestering carbon, addressing water use and redefining wastewater. It is important to ensure these spaces can be easily accessed and are healthy and inclusive for all to use.

Interior designers work widely with textiles, which can be complex in terms of regeneration. These textiles are often made with a combination of fibres that include petrochemical synthetic fibres (plastics) which are then impossible to separate and biodegrade. They also often use other petrochemicals in the form of humanmade artificial pesticides to grow crops such as non-certified, non-organic cotton, and have an accompanying high-level water footprint. Animal-fibre textiles may require chemical-intense crops to supplement the animals' feed, as well as having preservative chemicals added after manufacture to stop the living animal fibres from deteriorating, or to soften them and improve maintenance – and then are often blended with fossil-fuel synthetic fibres anyway. In some parts of the world, flame-retardant chemicals are also added to meet legal requirements for fire safety. These factors all prevent safe regeneration as the fibres reach their life-cycle end.

Pesticides were once acclaimed as a way of protecting crops and yields. Yet it is now widely recognised that they have negative impacts, as observed in biologist and environmentalist Rachel Carson's landmark book *Silent Spring*.[2] This book raised awareness after the author observed the damage caused to birds and the connected biodiversity in the years following World War II, when the use of chemical pesticides increased in agriculture following wartime government research. Her findings led to a US ban on dichloro-diphenyl-trichloroethane, more commonly known as DDT.

Sadly, all this time after Carson's findings, there are more harmful pesticides being used in agriculture than ever,[3] and DDT is still used in some countries where textiles are produced.[4] In the documentary film *The True Cost*, we are shown how hard it is for farmers with regards to pesticide use.[5] To meet demand, farmers in the Punjab are using genetically modified (GM) seed, tying themselves to the seed suppliers in order to fulfil crop demand and maximise yield. The GM cotton needs more pesticides, which then impact negatively on human health and biodiversity. The film also reports on LaRhea Peppe, a Texan cotton farmer who bucked the trend of her neighbouring farming communities and reverted to non-GM seed. As a regenerative farmer with an organic crop, she then formed a cooperative for organic cotton in her region. She has gone on to raise awareness by founding the Textile Exchange global non-profit to guide textile supply chains. While the film is broadly about the fashion industry, the parallels are there for all textile use.

Non-certified, non-organic cotton is one of the top environmentally damaging fabrics after acrylic, leather and silk.[6] It's a thirsty and dirty crop. A simple switch in specification to organically grown cotton, which looks identical but is farmed without synthetic pesticides and herbicides, comes with many benefits to biodiversity, including improved soil health, reduced water use and clean waterways. It has been estimated that the improved farming techniques involved in moving away from humanmade fertilisers would improve soil health and help to store enough carbon in the soil to keep the world within 1.5°C of global boiling.[7] The Global Organic Textile Standard (GOTS) looks at best practices for organic cotton and examines the effects on workers of the whole manufacturing process, from farm to factory. As well as better working conditions, GOTS certification means a minimum working age and a living wage.

Textiles are often made from synthetic fibres, often virgin and sometimes recycled using pre- or post-consumer waste or material retrieved from oceans, such as PET and abandoned fishing nets. While the recycling of plastic is good, both compositions are impossible to regenerate safely: plastic lives forever and sometimes contains human- and wildlife-impacting 'forever chemicals'. These non-regenerative, synthetic-fibre textiles, available to our industry in the form of fabrics and floor coverings, are now being seen as the new single-use plastics. In the UK, the Waste and Resources Action Programme (WRAP) carried out its first consumer research into home textiles and found the most frequently used disposal route for synthetic-fibre textiles is general rubbish, at 22%.[8]

Christine Gent, World Fair Trade Organization Fair Trade Expert and director of Fashion Revolution, said:

'Fabrics containing synthetic fibres are the new single-use plastic. I can understand why plastics can be used in medical use, but for fabrics we have so many beautiful alternatives to petrochemicals that we should never be using them ever again. I think every piece of cloth using these virgin fossil fuels should have a warning on the label that it is contributing to climate change. Let's look at everything, not just the warp and weft, the stitching; the zips and buttons, we just don't need to use petrochemical fossil fuels.'[9]

Two Sisters Ecotextiles

Seattle, USA

Unable to source a fabric to reupholster a sofa that was free of plastic or chemicals, sisters Patty Grossman and Leigh Anne Van Dusen joined forces and formed Two Sisters Ecotextiles, with a mission to 'change the way textiles are being made', by selling fabrics that are ethically produced, non-toxic, carbon neutral and otherwise sustainable. Their first collection debuted at UK interiors industry show Decorex in 2007. In their deeper research into the issues, the sisters made several discoveries that went on to inform their own framework for how their fabrics were assessed, from field to finished product, taking into account water use, chemical use, carbon footprint and plastic use. They had quickly identified in current fabric production that water, chemicals, energy and plastic are used in huge amounts by the industry. Pollution is increasingly a problem globally, as production often expels wastewater into waterways without any treatment, therefore contaminating groundwater, wildlife and ecosystems. It generally takes up 20 gallons of water to produce one yard of upholstery fabric. The sisters identified that 6,000 to 8,000 chemicals are used in fabric production. The German environment protection agency found that, by weight, fabric is made up of one quarter synthetic chemicals. Routinely, toxic chemicals are used such as cadmium, formaldehyde, arsenic, phthalates, benzene and benzidine and polyvinyl chlorine (PVC). The sisters saw there was little protection from the US government as regulators must prove a chemical is harmful to have it removed from the market.

Another concern was the carbon footprint of the life cycle of textile production. Grossman and Van Dusen discovered that while the focus is on concrete, timber, glass, steel and concrete used within the built environment, the per-kilogram embodied energy of fossil fuel derived polyester, acrylic and nylon used in textiles inside those spaces is far higher. They realised the scale of the plastic problem in the textile industry, noting that recycled plastic is still 'forever' and 'plastic'.

In order to truly ensure their fabrics were holistically safe and healthy, the sisters took on the responsibility of the design, sourcing

and manufacture of their fabric, ensuring they had nature-positive compositions. Insisting on 100% organically farmed native crops meant a lessened yield but it came with the important benefit of boosting soil health and therefore biodiversity, so leading to a reduced risk of drought, a reduced water footprint and reduced emissions of greenhouse gases. It even meant the soil became a carbon sink for removing carbon from the atmosphere.

Working directly with weavers, Grossman and Van Dusen evaluated there was little difference in energy use between weaving different fibre types, but the organically farmed fibres had a lesser impact through the next stage of textile processing, such as in the use of water and the management of wastewater discharge.

The issue of the water footprint of non-organic cotton production was highlighted in the BBC documentary 'Fashion's Dirty Secret',[10] where we saw how the once-huge inland Aral Sea in Kazakhstan had shrunk as the source water had been diverted for the huge cotton farms. The exposé also showed the chemical waste during textile manufacturing in the region of the Citarum River in Indonesia, where mercury, cadmium, lead and arsenic are present in the water used by neighbouring communities to bathe in and wash clothes.

Not being able to source locally as much as they'd hoped, the sisters' careful search for partners has taken them to many different parts of the world for their collection of safe and transparent fabrics: to Romania for hemp; a mill in Chile that was shifting to all-green processes; an Italian mill that had no wastewater in its process; a Japanese miller using ozone to bleach fabric instead of harmful chemicals; and an Italian dye house using heavy-metal-free, biodegradable textiles.

4.1 GOTS-certified 100% organic cotton velvet 'Methow', commissioned and sold by Two Sisters Ecotextiles.

FACTS

Founded: 2007

Founders: Patty Grossman, Leigh Anne Van Dusen

Awards: Green Log Homes & Lifestyle Awards™ 2009, BuildingGreen Top 10 Product 2008, *House and Garden Magazine* Best Merchandise Award 2007

Certifications: GOTS (the Global Organic Textile Standard) 50% of range; OEKO TEX® Made in Green 20% of range

Visit: Showroom (appointment only), 1605 South 93rd Street, Unit ED, Seattle, WA 98108, USA, www.twosistersecotextiles.com

4.2 GOTS-certified 100% organic cotton velvet 'Methow', in emerald green.

4.3 GOTS-certified 100% organic linen 'Bainbridge' in spring green and lined with cocoa.

4.4 Luca Alessandrini's 'Peel' chandelier, made from 'Orb' organic refuse bio-compound sheet material.

Biohm

London, UK

Bio-manufacturing company Biohm create safely compostable materials which avoid causing harm by cleverly replicating nature, a form of biomimicry, in the creation of their material innovations. Founder Dr Ehab Sayed was concerned about the impact of waste, and during his Masters study he discovered that the waste streams in the construction industry were poorly managed and particularly harmful.

Biohm's laboratory grows mycelium, the root system of fungi, a carbon sequestering, naturally fire-retardant alternative to non-regenerative petrochemical insulation board and acoustic insulation, which is currently being licensed to 200 factories globally at a cost viable to compete with the petrochemical equivalents used by the construction industry.

The laboratory is experimenting with mycelium grown using a food source of human hair collected in hairdressers and also recycled face masks, and has even found a strain of mycelium that can consume four types of plastic. It's experimenting with site waste streams including grass, oyster shells and champagne corks from Glyndebourne Opera House in the UK for Baker Brown Architects.

As well as functional uses, Biohm's regenerative materials can be turned into beautiful objects, such as Luca Alessandrini's 'Peel' chandelier made from 'Orb' organic refuse bio-compound. Here, the mycelium is fed with agricultural or food waste and then grown into board, or moulded. In this instance, orange peel was used, capturing the waste product at point of compost or landfill and catapulting its value to a long and appreciated new life, here as decorative lighting. The Orb material is made without a binder, any additives or coatings. However they are used, the materials developed by Biohm are designed to circulate back into waste streams with ease, free from synthetic additives, as a regenerative system.

Wonder-material mycelium has even been found to self-repair and regenerate.[11] Researchers have found engineered living material mycelium to self-heal holes in just two days in the leather-like grown substrate, which opens up lots of potential commercially as a self-repairable, in-use material.

FACTS

Founded: 2016

Founder: Dr Ehab Sayed

Awards: Recycled Product of the Year Award, National Recycling Awards 2023 (Obscure); Mixology22 Product of the Year Finalist: Lighting (Obscure); INDEX: Award 2021 – Work category

Visit: www.biohm.co.uk

Dora Chair

São João da Madeira, Portugal

The issue of safely regenerating the materials we use is very present in the interior design industry, where we combine multiple materials together. Some materials are taken from nature, some have a complex composition. We fix them together with permanent fixings and toxically with glues and then coat in petrochemical finishes, only to find that they cannot be returned to nature's cycle without causing harm.

Dora is a simple and well-designed durable chair made from easily disassembled, compostable timber and cork components. The chair's design is inspired by the shapes of the local wine-producing Douro Valley region in Portugal, where the seat represents the soil, and the frame, the vines. The designers were keen to use the materials honestly and employ a palette of materials that represent Portuguese culture, such as osier willow, hemp and straw. Timber from sustainably managed forests is a very regenerative material when used with water-based glues and finishes. It's a carbon sink, storing the carbon absorbed from the atmosphere in the wood even when it's manufactured into a structure. The forests are well managed, so biodiversity thrives, and the risk of forest fires is greatly reduced. This stackable chair's solid timber frame is sustainably sourced Forestry Stewardship Council (FSC®) certified ash, oak or walnut with a comfortable composite cork seat. The cork is from *Quercus suber* cork oak trees grown in Alentejo in the south of Portugal. Cork is regenerative and rapidly renewable; it is hand harvested from the bark of the cork oak tree every nine years, a process which is even found to increase the carbon absorption ability of the tree.[12] Cork is stain resistant, antibacterial, washable, non-toxic, waterproof and a great insulator, so it works well as a comfortable seat for this chair as the seat is warm in winter and cool in the summer. DAM's entire furniture range is custom-made to order to reduce any likelihood of waste.

4.5 Dora chair, based on the terrain of the local wine-growing region.

4.6 Dora chair, part of a series of furniture designs using local cork, designed by DAM's founders, Joana Santos and Hugo Silva. '

Joana Santos and Hugo Silva, co-founders of DAM, explained:

'Since the beginning, our purpose is to promote the storytelling about Portugal and the Sustainability. On the one hand, we want to contribute to the promotion of the Portugal brand, renewing a collective heritage that stays genuine and building the bridge between Culture and Economy. On the other hand, we are against the massification of products and consumerism; we believe in timeless and quality products. And it's imperative that people have more sustainable habits.'

FACTS

DAM Furniture

Founded: 2013

Founders: Joana Santos, Hugo Silva

Visit: Oliva Creative Factory, Rua da Fundição 240, 3700-119 São João da Madeira, Portugal, www.damportugal.com

Burwood Brickworks

Melbourne, Australia

How do we ensure our projects flourish and revive while fulfilling the traditional brief for the spaces and buildings that interior designers work with? Who writes the brief and where is nature in the design process?

Recognising that incremental change is no longer enough when faced with so little time to realign our ecological footprint to be within the planet's capacity, the non-profit International Living Future Institute (ILFI) has developed a wide span of tools to use to certify products, projects and communities. This includes The Living Building Challenge® (LBC) 'Living' and 'Petal' certifications, along with toolkits for working with developers and at municipal level, where there might be resistance. ILFI's founder Jason McLennan used the representation of a flower to demonstrate the framework for self-sufficiency – receiving water from the sky, energy from the sun, nutrients from the soil, providing a shelter for organisms and part of the ecosystem. The flower's petals represent each performance area. With their thought-provoking motto, 'What does good look like?', ILFI's priorities are to decarbonise the built environment and to make affordable housing more equitable – working on a broad range from buildings (refit, retrofit and new build), to infrastructure, neighbourhoods, landscapes and communities (urban and rural). LBC is simply known as a sustainability programme, but it's really an excellent example of regenerative sustainability where the bar is raised higher than merely maintaining a current level, with replenishment and restoration being more vital factors. One especially beautiful element is that a core part is to actively educate in the form of tours, case studies, operations manuals, brochures, signage and websites as a catalyst for change, with the prime aim being to get visitors asking, 'Why isn't every building like this?' and encouraging others to follow suit.

A project in Melbourne's suburbs shows how regenerative design can even take the form of a shopping centre. On an 18ha former brickworks site that stood derelict for 20 years, there now sits a

4.7 The north-facing, pot-plant wall of the medical centre at Burwood Brickworks, with reclaimed bricks, comprising 260 medium-sized citrus trees. The south-facing façade of the medical centre has shade-loving plants, including strawberries.

special scheme that not only revives and delights aesthetically but is an important LBC 'Petal-certified' regenerative project, forming a community of retail, leisure, parkland and 750 homes. The catalyst came from property development company Frasers Property Australia. Their project goal for the Burwood Brickworks site was human delight and the celebration of culture, spirit and place, and to be the world's most sustainable shopping centre, something they achieved at the time of receipt of the LBC Petal certification.

4.8 The saw-tooth roof spans 1,700m² and features artwork by Wurundjeri artist Mandy Nicholson, who also created artwork for the building's façade. The black-and-white design represents Victoria's indigenous carving culture and the six elements of – forest, sky, wind, water, on country and below country.

The shopping centre houses all the shops and services you'd expect to see, such as an off licence, barbers, beauty and hair salons, supermarket, a yoga and Pilates studio, chemist and medical centre, childcare centre, community space plus a six-screen cinema.

A vital part of the LBC process is to examine the land the project sits on and its history and to revive and celebrate it. Here, it is recognised that the Wurundjeri People had maintained and cared for the land for millennia. Since the 1900s, it had been orchards and market gardens and from the late 1930s it became a brickworks with a quarry.

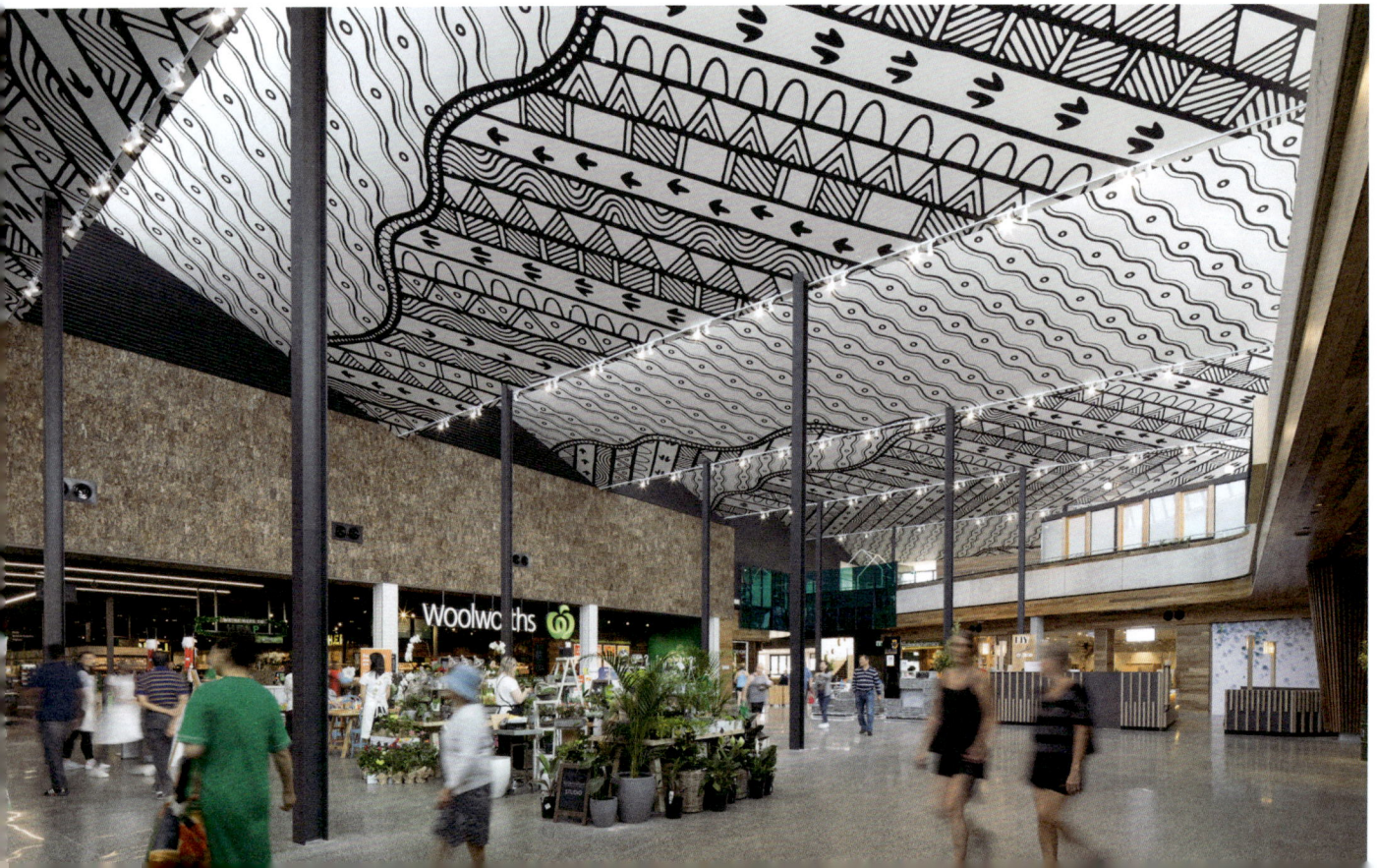

4.9 The rooftop urban farm, with outdoor dining areas.

4.10 A walkway leading to the market hall.

Biophilic design principles feature throughout the Burwood Brickworks project. The LBC process requires a series of charrette one-day workshops including all stakeholders, including designers, contractors, consultants and the client, to integrate the project with a biophilic design. As well as visual connection to nature and its textures, fresh air can enter the building via operable windows and natural daylight is optimised for comfort and wellness. Project interior designers Russell & George even designed indigenous- and biophilic-themed 'smellscapes' and soundscapes to connect to the place: the main entrance has an indigenous theme: there's a citrus-themed feature staircase and an earthy, woody-themed travellator. Indoor air quality is monitored, with limits in place for volatile organic compounds (VOCs) and provision of large entrance matting within airlock entrances to prevent particulates being brought into the interior. The focus on indoor air quality even comes down to ensuring the cleaning products used to maintain the building are not impacting the air quality.

On the roof is a working urban farm with 2,500m² of vertical and horizontal space for on-site food growing, which uses composted organic waste collected from tenants. The farm even has a run for rescued chickens. The farm serves as an outdoor classroom for local schools as well as other education establishments, community groups and local care homes, educating on food production. There's a wide variety of green spaces and parkland around the site, complete with 500 native trees and 100 types of native, pollinating plant species, plus a further 5,000m² of urban agriculture. No petrochemical pesticides or fertilisers are used. Blue spaces in the form of ponds have utilised former quarry areas. In addition, the developers contributed to the Living Future's Habitat Exchange, purchasing and protecting remote land in Argentina that is habitat to many animals, including the endangered Andean cat.

The building's design encourages activity: the staircase is central and easy to access. There are 200 bicycle storage spaces, along with showers, lockers and changing areas for the centre's staff and visitors, as well as electric charging points.

The building is powered net positively by clean energy from rooftop solar photovoltaic panels and off-site renewable energy, with gas installed only for commercial cooking where absolutely needed. Efficient water-saving fittings are used. Rain, storm and wastewater is all captured and treated for toilet flushing, washing machines, cooling towers, car washing and irrigation, and treated without

4.11 An area clad in reclaimed timber, leading to the market hall.

4.12 An travelator leading to the cinema entrance, complete with olfactory and sound experiences. The area is clad in reclaimed timber, including suspended pieces hanging from the ceiling, designed by interior designers Russell & George.

4.13 Dining space with lots of reclaimed materials.

chemicals using a membrane aerated bioreactor (MABR), the first to be installed in Australia, which sits underneath the underground car park.

During construction, 99% of building waste was diverted from landfill. Much of the operational waste-management plan includes closed-loop initiatives, such as source separation of materials; the site includes composting facilities, a dehydrator for food waste and worm farms.

The certification of this shopping centre extends to all its tenants, who also need to follow the principles and have a representative on the committee to monitor the performance of the building. All materials used were scrutinised and had to be non-toxic to the environment, food chain, supply chain workers, installers and users of the spaces, ensuring no ingredients were on the LBC 'Red List', such as formaldehyde, bisphenol-A, lead, mercury and PVC. Frasers Property Australia produced a 'Greensheet' of pre-approved products to further assist its tenants' design specifications. The timber used is 90% reclaimed and salvaged materials and products, as FSC®-certified timber sources were limited in Australia. The demand for FSC®-certified timber has since helped increase its availability in the country. To receive the LBC Petal certification, materials needed to be as locally sourced as possible, with a minimum of 20% of the materials construction budget from within 2,000km and 30% from within 5,000km. The majority of the building's construction budget was spent in Australia. Within LBC, points are scored for using third-party-screened 'Declare' label products. The demand resulting from this project has now meant Declare is established in Australia, with more than 40 products available.

Tenants resourcefully used salvaged light fittings, doors, bricks, basins, mirrors, shelving and cladding. They reused flooring, chose mechanically fixed carpet tiles rather than permanent glues, repurposed bottles as lighting fixtures and sourced mycelium lighting, crushed glass flooring and shopfront signage made from moss. There were operational improvements as well, such as a water refill station rather than selling plastic bottled water. Crockery is used rather than single-use packaging, moving sales from bottled products to refillable. Many of the tenants are larger chains and these improvements have sent ripples through their business models, supply chains and future projects following this learning experience. Contractors have learnt a great deal about alternative materials, supply chains and skills, and have new relationships within the industry.

Regular tours of the building and open days take place to educate the community and pass on learnings to other building projects. Frasers Property Australia's Greensheet is freely available. Retailers have reported lower-than-average staff turnover. The project has also achieved the Greenstar Communities certification from the Green Building Council of Australia. While the shopping centre has achieved LBC Petal certification, the developers are continuing to fulfil the extra requirements for it to be fully LBC certified, complete with post-occupancy monitoring and evaluation.

For Frasers Property Australia, biophilic design, healthier materials and solar farms are now included in their retail projects as standard. From a marketing perspective, would the world know about this project if it hadn't followed this regenerative course?[13]

FACTS

Interior design: Russell & George and NH Architecture

Architect: NH Architecture

Interior architect: Zwei Architecture – Urban Farm Restaurant and Café

Certification: The Living Building Challenge® Petal Certified v. 3.1. Petals: Place, Health and Happiness, Biophilic environment, Materials, Equity, Beauty.

Completion: 2019

Gross internal floor area: 18,568m2

Visit: Burwood Brickworks, 70 Middleborough Road, Burwood East, VIC 3151, Australia, www.burwoodbrickworks.shopping

explore

Frasers Property Australia, 'Greensheet', www.frasersproperty.com.au/A-Different-Way/LBC-Greensheet

International Living Future Institute, the Living Building Challenge®, www.living-future.org

William McDonough and Michael Braungart, *The Upcycle: Beyond Sustainability – Designing for Abundance*, North Point Press, 2013.

Jason McLennan, 'Living buildings for a living future', TEDxBend, Bend, Oregon, USA, May 2015.

Textile Exchange, www.textileexchange.org

Untold Creative, *The True Cost*, documentary film, 2016, www.truecostmovie.com

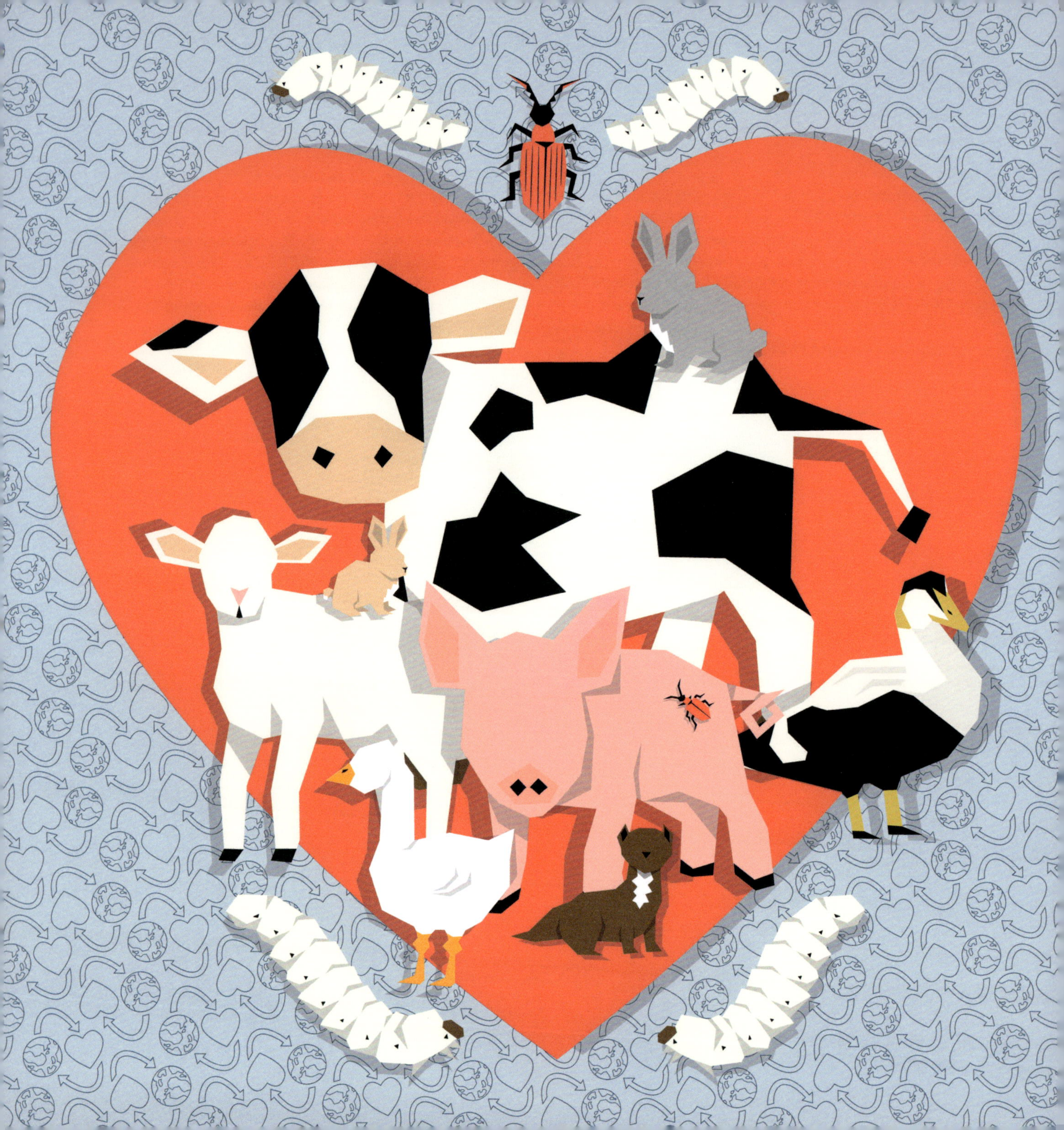

5

Vegan Design

My own journey into vegan design was an extension of the ethos learnt during my time from the mid-1990s working as a designer for Anita Roddick's The Body Shop International's headquarters. The company's ethics included respect for the animal kingdom, as well as for people and for the planet. As part of the company's conscious-sourcing policy, it avoided the use of animal-derived products not only in its skin and bodycare retail offering but also in the materials used in the built environment for the company. When you list animal-derived products, you realise how many ways they surround us — leather, suede, skins, wool, silk, down, feathers, bone, fur, shell. Some paints, finishes and adhesives may be animal tested or have animal product content; beeswax, lanolin and other coatings and additives also include animal products. Roddick showed the world that business could prosper without the need to exploit. Her business operated with respect for the fellow inhabitants of our planet in the animal kingdom, and did not use them as commodities. I learnt that we were part of nature and should respect it. Of course, there were occupant health benefits to this way of specifying through avoiding toxic chemicals, too, which was also of great importance to Roddick's wellness business.

This ethos of avoiding animal products evolved in the interior design (and fashion design) industry, known more recently as vegan design, with pioneering interior designer Deborah DiMare in North America and interior architect Aline Dürr in Australia leading the way by each producing training courses and books to educate their industry. Both designers reveal the grim realities present in some parts of the interior design industry's supply chains and highlight the many ways — some obvious and many less so — that animal products are used in processes, products, materials and finishes. Not all producers in the interior design industry's supply chain are the same; there are always exceptions, but generally large-scale commerce and animals prove not to mix well.

It has been interesting to observe how the use of the word 'vegan' in relation to this methodology and approach to specifying interiors has been received. As the vegan movement has grown, the word has become so firmly connected to dietary choices that the use of it has become intertwined and complex. However, it is the correct term, which is why I've used it. Vegan means 'produced without exploiting animals in any way'.[1] 'Cruelty Free' is sometimes used as a softer and less diet-related term, but Cruelty Free really only means 'developed without being tested on animals',[2] which obviously is a good thing, but is not the same as a product or material that is guaranteed not to include ingredients derived from animals. There is much debate over the labelling of non-food products as vegan. If misused, these can greenwash and falsely reassure, as while the products might omit animal ingredients, they may be toxic in other ways or use fossil fuels.

Of course, you don't need to be vegan to work without using animal products in interior design. To begin with, my avoidance of using animal products in my design work did not correlate with my lifestyle, although I did gradually become vegan over the next two decades. I'm not sure exactly when the term 'vegan design' began to be used: early in my career it was about asking suppliers for transparency and making subsequent relatively simple swaps in specifications, coming from increased awareness of animal treatment in our industry and the planetary and health impacts.

Apart from compassionate reasons, it's good business sense to have awareness of the issues and the alternatives. Designers would be savvy to keep up with this shift in ethical consumerism. Many of our clients are increasingly aware of the issues and are exploring more ethical sources for all aspects of their lives, wanting to live a life without exploiting animals or the planet or people. Many everyday consumers routinely avoid animal-tested toiletries and cleaning products but are not vegan. As we have more access to information and become more informed on what happens in some supply chains, it is hard to ignore some of the realities that exist.

My own motivation comes from being a voice for the voiceless. We have an opportunity to be on the right side of history as future generations look back at the disconnection from our fellow living beings who coexist on this beautiful planet — our speciesism, in fact — alongside our poor treatment of fellow humans and the planet. Moving away from the negativity, it's such an exciting time to embrace and celebrate change. Thanks to pioneering businesses and research and development in the apparel and automotive industries, we have

5.1 The vegan hotel suite at Hilton London Bankside designed by Bompas & Parr

access to so much exciting and positive Next Generation material innovation, much of which is part of the circular economy. We no longer need to look to the animal kingdom for materials in the way our ancestors did.

In 2019, the 'world's first vegan suite' was revealed at the Hilton's London Bankside hotel. Designed by international multisensory experiential designers Bompas & Parr, the suite caused a huge stir, attracting global press interest. It was such a great landmark project for vegan design as it demonstrated the many ways that not just an interior could be animal free but also the whole guest experience. Working with The Vegan Society, every detail of this experience was considered – glues, inks, dyes, fibres – from the dedicated vegan specified check-in desk furniture, stationery and key card, through to the toiletries and food and drink, for both room service and a dedicated area of the hotel's OXBO restaurant. The suite has organic cotton carpets, bamboo floors and pineapple leather upholstery. Instead of the usual wool and feather-stuffed bed and bedding, vegan alternatives were used, such as organic buckwheat, bamboo fibres, kapok or millet hulls. Guests can choose from a plant-based pillow menu. The rooms are even cleaned and laundered with vegan products. The suite continues to be very popular with guests, whether vegan or not, but the concept is yet to be repeated elsewhere in the hotel group.

Named after the Scottish Gaelic word for Freedom, the 11-bedroom, dog-friendly, baronial Saorsa 1875 hotel has 100% vegan food and drink, with seasonal menus made from ingredients grown in the hotel's two acres of grounds, as well as foraged and local produce. All furnishings and bedding are animal free and the hotel is powered by 100% renewable and animal-waste-free Ecotricity, which is certified vegan by The Vegan Society and vegan charity Viva! The family-owned and operated hotel business concept is due to expand to other locations in the future.

5.2 The Hilton project was quickly followed by the UK's first 100% vegan hotel, Saorsa 1875 in Pitlochry, in Scotland's Highlands. The check in desk at Saorsa 1875.

5.3 The cocktail bar at Saorsa 1875.

Why are animal products so associated with luxury? It seems our notion of luxury has become seriously flawed. When paying premium prices, we assume that remuneration flows through the supply chain, along with high welfare for people and animals. Filmmaker Rebecca Cappelli's feature documentary 'Slay' (2022) goes behind the scenes of the global leather industry to look at its impact. Animal cruelty and sweatshops are not luxurious. How did the trade of animal skins become such a perceived luxury? Exposés like Cappelli's, PETA's (People for the Ethical Treatment of Animals) and numerous more reveal the dire conditions for both the animals and the workers, often alongside abuse of the environment, as well.[3] What really stayed with me from Deborah DiMare's vegan design course was seeing the life of tannery workers in Bangladesh.[4] They experience poor pay, long working hours wading barefoot in toxic chemicals, and 90% of workers have an estimated 50-year life expectancy.[5] Meanwhile, the hidden human cost to this animal supply chain is people from the surrounding community, who eat from the chemical-polluted waterways and soil, and breathe the polluted air.

Upon learning about the many issues of the animal leather industry, Helen Farr-Leander, founder of the luxury accessories brand Watson & Wolfe, transitioned to working with innovative, non-animal leathers such as cork, corn and cactus and sourcing manufacturers who were environmentally conscious but also treated their workers with respect, paying them fairly and providing safe working conditions. She and her supply chain were part of the global Fashion Revolution campaign, making the workers visible, promoting cultural and industry change and lobbying for governmental policy change to enforce laws and regulate the industry. Farr-Leander said:

'Luxury is defined as something which is inessential, desirable or expensive. Luxury is not a material, it encapsulates design, craftsmanship, quality of materials, respect for people and social responsibility. Would a leather wallet on a market stall produced in a sweatshop be perceived as Luxury, simply because it is made from animal leather?

Crocodile skin is considered luxurious, but the process to obtain the skin is barbaric. The brands who use this material shroud themselves with their luxury label and charge big prices for these items. So now we are led to believe that abhorrent cruelty is also Luxury.

Next-generation leather alternatives are engineered, but that doesn't make them less desirable or less expensive. And it should depend entirely on how the material is used, how it is crafted and how the final product looks as to whether it is Luxury. Luxury is being redefined. Soon, it will no longer promote waste, pollution, cruelty and high levels of CO2e in the supply chain, it will embrace sustainability, organic materials, recycling and the circular economy.' [6]

While I want to demonstrate positive work in this book to inspire, I probably should tackle the two recurring arguments that happen when vegan alternatives are discussed.

The first is about leather. It's often argued that polyurethane (PU) leather substitutes are environmentally worse than animal leather. In response, I would argue:

a   Yes, some faux leathers are made of polyurethane, a fossil-fuel-derived petrochemical. However, there are very many animal leather alternatives that are not petrochemical based. Most followers of a vegan lifestyle are nature loving and would want to avoid toxic chemicals and petrochemicals as well as animal cruelty. Hence the surge in popularity of food-waste leathers available now, such as apple, pineapple, cactus and mushroom, supporting the circular economy while attempting to address the huge issue of society's food waste.

b   While I'm not endorsing PU leather, findings[7] show that animal leather is far more harmful than PU leather in terms of greenhouse gas emissions, including carbon (CO_2e).

c   The argument never considers how an animal might feel about all this.

Regardless of those three things, the PU leather / animal leather argument does raise a number of issues – of chemical use, the perception of natural and the concept of by-products. There are also further issues of land use, water use and greenhouse gas emissions, including methane (CH_4) and carbon dioxide (CO_2). When it comes to animal products, 100% natural is an unlikely reality when you consider these are deteriorating animal parts that need preservative chemicals to prevent them from rotting.

The second argument is about using perceived 'by-products' as resources that would otherwise go to waste. I, too, believed this, but not all by-products are equal. This seems to be another misconception that artificially keeps us at ease using animal products by reframing and moving the blame and guilt to the meat industry instead. Leather is a valuable industry and, in some cases, it could be said that meat is the by-product of the leather industry. Meat and skins are co-products; leather is a huge, profit-driven industry of its own.[8] A study even shows it's better for the environment to leave skins to rot in landfill than to prepare and tan them.[9] Sheep did not always need to be sheared. It's been argued they only need shearing because they have been bred to produce excessive wool.[10] With down, it is very difficult to transparently trace its chain of custody reliably; it is often live harvested, as is angora and cashmere, which causes much pain and distress to the animal. PETA's exposé on the mohair industry resulted in many brands, including interior designer Kelly Hoppen, banning the use of mohair in their products.

According to Sascha Camilli, vegan fashion writer, speaker and educator, founder of digital vegan fashion magazine *Vilda* and author of *Vegan Style: Your Plant-Based Guide to Fashion, Beauty, Home and Travel*:

'Most people believe in being compassionate and respecting animals – they just need to take the step to bridge that gap between their morals and how they live their lives. This is where education and awareness play an important role: many consumers aren't conscious of vegan products beyond food. Once they learn about the cruelty inherent in the industries which exploit animals and realise that high-quality alternatives exist, living in alignment with their values becomes a no-brainer.'[11]

MIRUM®

Peoria, Illinois, USA

Back to the innovation, excitingly there is much happening in the world of high-performing materials, and products with many of the properties of leather are coming onto the market. These alternatives are derived from nature and most commonly utilise food crop waste, such as pineapple (Piñatex®), apple (Leap™), nut shells (Kudarat), cactus (Desserto), grape skins (VEGEA), cork, mycelium (Forager Hides), mushroom (Mylo), agricultural waste, forestry waste (Polybion), persimmons (Persiskin), banana skins (Banofi) and even flowers (Fleather).

MIRUM® is not only 100% bio-based, but also fully circular and produced using renewable energy. Used for footwear, fashion, automotive upholstery and accessories, MIRUM® is an entirely animal-free 'alt leather' material, made with Forestry Stewardship Council (FSC®) certified natural rubber, cork and charcoal, as well as coir, clays, plant-based oils and waxes. Unlike most leather alternatives, it's completely plastic-free and is United States Department of Agriculture (USDA) 'BioPreferred' approved, thanks to it being 100% bio-based, composed of a combination of virgin natural materials and upcycled, carbon-sequestering agricultural side-stream by-products. It can be customised to look like leather or carbon fibre, so has a broad creative palette for how it can be used. Its TENCEL™ backing is cellulose-based with plastic-free fibres, making the final product reusable and completely biodegradable.

For compassionate and environmentally conscious handbag and accessories manufacturer Veshin, who makes products for luxury global brands, avoiding animal leather and petrochemical ingredients has been the constant aim. Founder Joey Pringle has closely followed the development of progressive, next-generation alternative leathers coming to market. Veshin was an early adopter of MIRUM®. Pringle described to me the similarity of the feel and grain to animal leather, properties that are vitally important to his clients. This 100% plastic-free and safely regenerative material not only meets the aims

5.4 A Veshin cushion made from MIRUM® next-generation leather.

5.5 A Veshin toiletry bag made from MIRUM® next-generation leather.

of Pringle's ethical company but also the demands and high standards of its discerning customers, who expect high performance but also want to avoid animal leather. Simply labelling a 'less bad' PU non-animal leather as vegan is just not enough for them.

FACTS

MIRUM® / Natural Fiber Welding, Inc

Founded: 2015

Founder: Dr Luke Haverhals

Awards: Winner of Fast Company's World's Most Innovative Companies: Style (March 2022), Energy & Sustainability (March 2023); Conservation X Labs Microfiber Innovation Challenge (March 2022); PETA Fashion Awards 2022 – Innovation Award; PETA Fashion Innovation Award 2022

Certifications: MIRUM® is a USDA-certified 100% bio-based material

Visit: www.mirum.naturalfiberwelding.com

Waterfront Residence

Miami, USA

American TV interior designer and animal-lover Deborah DiMare had a realisation that changed her life. She had already changed her diet, spurred on after researching with her family the treatment of animals and then discovering the annual dog-meat-eating festival in the Chinese city of Yulin.[12] Shortly afterwards, she discovered that the term 'leather' in China was not only bovine, but potentially cat and dog skins as well.[13] Horrified at the prospect she could be inadvertently buying those leather products for herself and her clients, her values quickly led from her plate to her wardrobe, and then to her interior design business, which she completely pivoted after working in the industry for more than 10 years.

5.7 The lounge at DiMare's Miami residence.

DiMare found herself being quizzed by animal-loving fellow designers on her research into animal-free alternatives, so she started to work closely with PETA on developing an industry-accredited course to educate the interior design industry by using PETA's undercover investigations to demonstrate the treatment of animals and conditions for workers in the industry.

As DiMare said in her podcast interview with LuAnn Nigara, 'I believe that luxury design should look good, feel good and do good.'[14]

At the same time, DiMare realised the health benefits for her clients of using the alternatives, helping allergy sufferers, and those living with autism and sensory issues, through creating non-toxic, compassionate interiors. Focusing on the wellness benefits of avoiding animal products has been the focus for her team's work at DiMare Design and is something for which DiMare's business is globally known. She happily

5.8 The principal bedroom at the Miami home.

calls herself an animal activist and uses her platforms and connections to educate and share her knowledge widely.

DiMare explained, 'Our home should reflect who we are, bring out the best in us, and contribute to a better world.'[15]

When designing the waterfront Miami home for her family, it was critical to DiMare that there was 'no blood, despair or tragedy attached to it'. Seeing the use of animal products today as archaic, she took what she had learnt about the negative impacts of the interior design industry and instead filled her home with positive luxurious materials that supported her family's health. She used texture and relief to make their home feel sensory and tactile.

For years, DiMare had used animal products in projects and had found herself saying things to clients that she now sees as indicators of chemicals being present in materials, such as telling clients when choosing a leather bed headboard not to have one if they didn't like the smell and suggesting a soft fabric instead. Recognising how much time we spend in bed and also quite how many of the materials used in bedrooms are animal materials, she focused on designing and specifying healthy bedrooms, creating a textural, sensory experience to promote good sleep and wellbeing. Her research found several possible toxins could be present in bedroom specifications, including phthalates, per- and polyfluoroalkyl substances (PFAS), known as 'forever chemicals', and flame retardants. She worked to avoid these, recognising that sleep is restorative and should not be harmful.

Even though health and ethics were of great concern, DiMare ensured comfort was an equally important factor. Instead of using silk or down or wool, she used banana silk, kapok, pesticide-free hemp, buckwheat, bamboo and TENCEL™. She strongly feels the 'responsible' label is not reliable when buying down or wool and prefers to find alternatives. She works collaboratively with her suppliers to source healthy and humane solutions, using third-party certifications such as the Global Organic Textile Standard (GOTS) and OEKO-TEX® to navigate the market and avoid toxic chemical use.

DiMare's human-centred approach combines conscious specifications with feng shui and biophilic design. It's unsurprising

that an animal-loving designer who wants to avoid animal cruelty and toxic chemicals would connect firmly to place and to the beauty of the natural world in their work. DiMare's designs draw inspiration from the forms, sounds, smells and feelings that nature-positive design encompasses, complete with interacting with, watching and listening to wildlife to support her clients' wellbeing.

DiMare loves to inject her designs with joyful pieces of furniture, like the hanging chair (pictured) made without animals or chemicals. She also uses positive reminders of people or experiences – items to make her clients feel good.

She explained, 'I was designing interiors with animal-based furniture for many years. However, once I opened my eyes to the truth, I could no longer support an industry that kills creatures, human and non, while destroying our planet. Those are the facts, as harsh as they seem, and why I transitioned my interior design business to be 100% vegan and humane.'[16]

FACTS

Interior design: DiMare Design

Completion: 2019

Gross internal floor area: 836m²

5.9 The bathroom.

5.10 The dining room features a locally felled tree root used as a table base.

5.11 A hanging chair in the waterfront residence.

WEGANOOL™

Faborg Auroville, India

The Vegan Homeware Awards were created in 2016 by PETA to showcase and reward progress and innovation in the industry, an international recognition for products, books and designers avoiding the use of animal products. Both Deborah DiMare and Aline Dürr have received awards. The annual awards are judged by the PETA headquarters team and are often based on feedback from their supporters.
The awards have been received by international press including *The Independent, House Beautiful, Ideal Home* and *Interiors Monthly.*

A previous winner of PETA's Fashion Innovation Award which is also relevant to the interior design industry is WEGANOOL™, a plant-based, chemical-free, wool alternative made from 25% stem and 5% pod fibres of the *Calotropis gigantea* plant, combined with 70% organic, rain-fed cotton. The plant thrives in drought-prone and depleted soils, needs very little water and no fertiliser or pesticides. Growing it restores soil fertility and biodiversity.

The biodegradable fabric developed by Faborg has been mostly utilised for garment making, as it has a similarity to cashmere and its hollow cellulose structure makes the woven fabric breathable and easy to maintain. The fabric feels warm, doesn't irritate the skin and is antimicrobial. Fabric innovator Faborg has made its processing system zero waste by using the biomass and effluent created through fibre extraction and the dyeing process as a natural fertiliser and pest repellent.

As well as having homeware, fashion and food awards (including the Fashion Innovation Award that was won by WEGANOOL™), PETA also has the 'PETA-Approved Vegan' logo – a certification used by over 1,000 brands to help consumers identify clothing, accessories and home furnishing items made from vegan alternatives.

Yvonne Taylor, PETA's Director of Corporate Projects, explained, 'Today's conscious consumers want designs that no animal had to be beaten, slaughtered or skinned for.'[17] Elisa Allen, Vice President of UK Programmes and Operations at PETA, said, 'PETA is celebrating the forward-thinking companies leading the way in vegan interior design.'[18]

FACTS

Founded: 2015

Founders: Gowri Shankar, Elen Tsopp

Awards: PETA Fashion Innovation Award 2020

Visit: www.faborg.in/weganool

explore

Sascha Camilli, *Vegan Style: Your Plant-Based Guide to Fashion, Beauty, Home and Travel,* Murdoch Books, 2019.

Deborah DiMare:

Deborah DiMare, *Vegan Interiors,* Blurb, 2018.

Vegan Design online course: www.vegandesign.lpages.co/vegan-design-101-course

Other shorter courses and resources: www.vegandesign.org/learn-vegan-design

Aline Dürr:

Aline Dürr, Vegan Interior Design, Lightning Source, 2020.

Course: The Vegan Interior Design Method, www.veganinteriordesign.com

'Fashion Reimagined', feature documentary, Together Films, 2022, www.fashionreimaginedfilm.com

Fashion Revolution: www.fashionrevolution.org

PETA Vegan Homeware Awards: www.peta.org.uk

'Slay', feature documentary, First Spark Media, 2022, www.slay.film

'The True Cost', feature documentary, Untold Creative, 2016, www.truecostmovie.com

5.12 WEGANOOL™, winner of PETA's Fashion Innovation Award 2022.

6

People

In 2022, the United Nations General Assembly recognised that everyone, everywhere, has the right to live in a clean, healthy and sustainable environment, meaning that for those in power respecting this is no longer an option but an obligation.'

WWF Living Planet Report, 2022[1]

Supply chains have impact on more than the planet. Our buying and specification choices can inadvertently cause harm to people as well as to the environment and the natural world. Interior designers may use something that is deemed renewable and safe to the planet, but it can still cause harm to people, so cannot be seen as truly sustainable. That harm can be identified upstream in our supply chains, exploiting those working to produce raw materials and goods in unsafe working conditions, inequity, poor pay or, worse still, forced, bonded or child labour.[1] The 'people' part of sustainability is often overlooked and it is happening in a multitude of ways. We use raw materials that are extracted, mined, grown and farmed. Manufacturing processes are complex. How do we make sure people aren't exploited in those processes?

Supply chains can impact the health of those communities living close to stages of production through toxic chemical pollution of soil, air or water.[2] Those downstream in the supply chain from us can also be exposed to health risks, through installing and working with materials interior designers regularly specify, and during materials' in-use stage there is potential for harming building occupants. Even firefighters are experiencing negative health effects as a result of materials burning and combining together in a toxic chemical soup.[3]

Our specifications can indirectly harm people living on the other side of the planet in already vulnerable communities through the effects of polluted air, water and soil, and the devasting impacts of increased global temperature, extreme weather events and rising sea levels.[4] Supply chains can exploit people and nature through using manufacturing in parts of the world where weaker laws exist, either directly through labour laws or by ones that neglect to protect the environment. The lifestyle of the wealthy Global North is at the expense of the Global South, from where we extract materials and manufactured goods, and then return them back as unwanted waste at the end of use, along with the climate heating and pollution that goes with it. This is not sustainable and is climate colonialism. The International Panel on Climate Change (IPCC) now connects climate change and colonialism in its reporting,[5] acknowledging that wealthy countries are continuing the history of exploitation, not just of natural resources, but also human ones.

We are purchasing things at the expense of others, whose labour has been exploited in the supply chain. The concept of a living wage provides some form of assurance to consumers, but it is not the same thing across the world. We rest easy when we see the words 'living wage', when in truth it's desperately basic for the Global South, compared to what is provided in richer countries. A living wage is such a basic thing to receive: giving the ability to buy food, pay rent, clothe yourself and pay for medical treatment when you need it. Yet many supply chains pay less than a living wage and capitalise on the desperation of workers, deeming their work low value and dividing labour so the tasks are so basic and repetitive that they do not impart any valuable skill to the worker. Fashion activism organisation Fashion Revolution found that only 2% of fashion workers globally are paid a liveable salary.[6] Ensuring a living wage means degrowth, and therefore helps us to live within planetary boundaries.

Safia Minney, social entrepreneur and author, explained:

'We need living wages to be central to the sustainability debate and action for the fashion industry. We need a Just Transition for the industry as we kick out the fossil fuel prop and we cut production significantly. Paying living wages will reduce the use and extraction of natural resources and destruction of our ecosystems and help us transition to ecological economics.'[7]

Safe working conditions were never more brought into focus than at Rana Plaza in Bangladesh, where, in 2013, the eight-storey factory building producing fast-fashion garments collapsed, with more than

3,000 people inside, killing 1,134 workers and maiming many of the survivors. On the day of this disaster, workers had seen cracks in the building and had evacuated but were told to work or they'd lose a month's pay. This building housed clothing factories producing garments for major fashion outlets used globally. Bangladesh is known to be one of the countries with the lowest wages and the fewest employment laws in the world.[8] The Rana Plaza collapse prompted the International Accord, an agreement for workplace health and safety protection signed by suppliers in the textiles and garment industry.

We need to be better aware of material safety at end-of-life stage – how we dispose of materials carefully, and know where 'away' really is. Domestic plastic waste, including textiles, is moved to developing countries where regulation is poor or non-existent. This is being referred to as waste colonialism. Trash | Track[9] was an experiment in Seattle where 3,000 everyday items were smart-tagged and put into the regular domestic recycling process, and tracked, with most being pretty swiftly exported to be dumped on communities in the Global South.

Every minute, one truckload of rubbish is being dumped in our oceans.[10] 'The Trash Isles'[11] was a name given to an area of plastic in the North Pacific which in 2018 was the size of France, to draw attention to the issue of dumped plastics in our oceans. It was made up from plastic that was dumped, and washed into oceans from waterways and fishing activities. As these plastics break down, they find their way into seafood, are ingested by humans[12] and cause economic loss to coastal communities.[13] It's so easy to think this is purely about single-use food packaging, but in the UK the construction industry is the second-largest user of plastic waste, generating an estimated 50,000 tonnes of plastic packaging waste each year.[14] UK non-profit initiative Changing Streams traces plastic pollution directly related to the construction industry and is raising awareness, educating and facilitating change in our industry. Its

founder, construction company owner Neal Maxwell, was horrified when on a trip of a lifetime to the Arctic he witnessed the high levels of plastic pollution there and set about raising awareness, drawing up a programme with the University of Liverpool to make the construction industry plastic-free by 2040.[15]

Maxwell warned:

> 'Never has it been so important to consider the materials we choose for building projects. Since the early 1950s, plastics have become the go-to products for a wide range of applications. Plastic production has grown exponentially over recent years, with over 400 million tonnes produced annually [worldwide]. Of this, 20% enters the construction industry, the second-largest user of plastic after the packaging industry.
>
> But there's a catch, and it's a big one! Plastic pollution is having a devastating effect on the planet, wildlife and marine life: only now are we starting to understand the impact it is having on human health as new scientific evidence emerges. Plastic that enters the supply chain today, particularly in the construction industry, becomes the plastic pollution of the future.'[16]

We need full transparency of true, clear, standardised information regarding materials and their chains of custody, which is secure, tamperproof and can stay with the material through its life. None of this is happening at significant scale in the competitive world of commerce, where there is unwillingness to disclose trade secrets and profit is the prime objective.

6.1 Hand-loom-woven textiles from Selyn Textiles, using locally sourced fibres from the community's own backyards.

The Embassy of the Kingdom of the Netherlands

Colombo, Sri Lanka

Selyn Textiles is a Sri Lankan social enterprise and brand, which has been supporting and empowering more than 1,000 female entrepreneur artisans who hand-weave truly natural, biodegradable traditional handloom textiles all across the island. Their PETA-approved fabrics (see Chapter 5) are free from any animal-derived products and use local waste plant fibres such as banana, coconut, palm, reed and jute. Their cotton fabrics use certified OEKO TEX® STANDARD 100 and GOTS-certified organic yarn (see Chapter 5) and are Bluesign and REACH certified for non-harmful dyes and chemicals.

Founded by Sandra Wanduragala in 1991, Selyn Textiles has been World Fair Trade Organization (WFTO) Fair Trade Guaranteed since 2008. This guarantees efficient and continued investment in communities, no child or forced labour, fair pay, and equitable and safe working conditions. The company is now run by Wanduragala's daughter Selyna Peris, who wanted to ensure their version of fair trade was robust and publicly transparent, especially faced with challenges within the supply chain during Covid-19. During this challenging time, they lost touch with some artisans in the supply chain, proving that transparency and digital connectivity is very important. So together with Bilal Bhatti of Swedish technology company PaperTale, they have now integrated blockchain technology for 'radical transparency' and traceability of the social and environmental impact created within their supply chain. This blockchain is secure, public and freely accessible via a consumer app. On the app, the whole flow of the social and environment data is securely recorded for the journey of the product through the supply chain process to customers. The weaver confirms all payments, there is information on processes, any dyes used, water footprint and any environmental impact, which is all independently verified and securely added to the blockchain for 100% transparency and traceability.

Bonnie Horbach, the Dutch ambassador to Sri Lanka and the Maldives, is an advocate for responsible and ethical business, through fair pay and recognition for the people creating valued and skilfully made products. Her wish is for producers in the Global South to sell directly and therefore reap the profits from their products. One of Horbach's first engagements in her new placement in the Sri Lankan embassy was to attend Selyn Textiles' launch of its blockchain initiative. She could see how valuable and innovative the project was for the island's artisans. It also connects closely to the discussion in the Netherlands, and in fact in the rest of the Global North, around decolonisation. In 2022, the Netherlands admirably became the first European country to make an apology for its role in the slave trade.[17] The Dutch government is recognising the injustices of its colonial past and is in a process of rectifying imbalances as a result of it.

The embassy building and ambassador's residence were about to be redesigned in collaboration with the Dutch government's in-house interior architect Nicole van der Velden. It was decided that these themes should be reflected in the interiors of the buildings. The project provided a great opportunity to collaborate with and showcase Selyn Textiles by using their fabrics in the refurbishment to reupholster existing furniture. Not only would this be in line with

6.2 Selyn Textiles' public blockchain app ensures transparency and traceability.

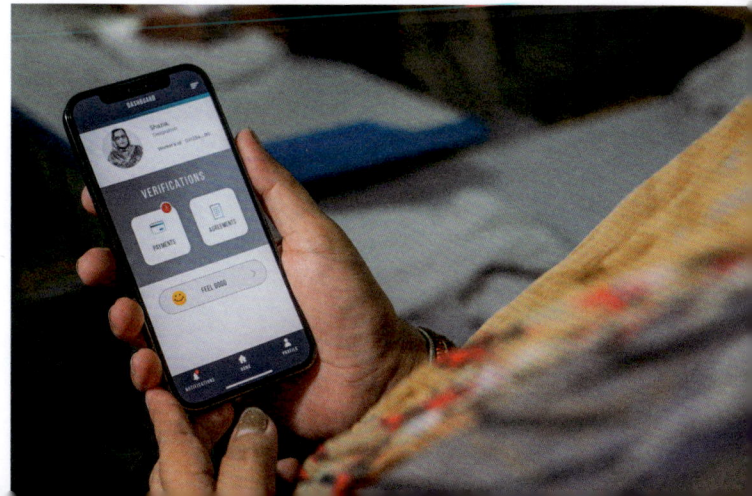

6.3 A seating area inside the embassy.

6.4 A boardroom inside the embassy.

the sustainability goals of the Dutch government, but it also tells the story about transparency of the supply chain, Responsible Business Conduct principles and, importantly, by doing so, the aspiration to decolonise relations, support a paradigm shift and truly equalise relations between the Global South and Global North; between the previously colonised and the colonisers; between the sellers and the buyers.

As the in-house designer, van der Velden works on the Dutch government's embassy and residence buildings across Asia, Australia and New Zealand. Over the years she has developed an approach to her design process. She does this by working very collaboratively with the stakeholders for each project to determine the brief, exchange ideas and deliver the concept. Van der Velden's objective always is to culturally connect to each location, showcase the Netherlands to visitors of the buildings, and share learnings and innovation for the environment through her designs.

During the design process, van der Velden selected unique and thought-provoking furniture, objects and soft furnishings. Working with the embassy's art curator, art by Dutch artists was selected, such as Saar Scheurlings's *Totem*, and used within the design scheme as talking pieces. The circular economy is essential in her methodology. Van der Velden selected colours from the Selyn Textiles range to reupholster existing furniture, much of which is by Dutch designers. Designs and products were used from Sri Lankan craftspeople and from Dutch companies including Occony, DUM Office and Ahrend, who produce modular, repairable products made from healthier materials. Any new additions to the buildings must be of high quality and last at least 16 years. Van der Velden and her colleagues were constantly challenging suppliers on ways to improve delivery packaging materials and all freight was by sea.

Bonnie Horbach explained:

> *After the refurbishment everything selected has meaning, has a story and has a place. For me as a diplomat, it is a visual reminder of what we want to accomplish. I am able to use the art and objects as a tool to begin discussions, reflect on our shared history and also to show what we can do together.*[18]

6.5 Working and seating areas inside the embassy.

FACTS

Client: Ambassador of the Kingdom of the Netherlands to Sri Lanka and the Maldives

Architect: Nicole van der Velden

Completion: 2023

Gross internal floor area – embassy: 625m²; residence: 210m²

SELYN TEXTILES

Founded: 1991

Founder: Sandra Wanduragala

Certifications: World Fair Trade Organization (WFTO) Fair Trade Guaranteed, PETA-Approved Vegan, OEKO TEX® and GOTS certified (cotton yarn), REACH and Bluesign certified (dyes and chemicals)

Awards: Redress Design Award 2021; Sandra Wanduragala received 'Forbes 50 over 50 Asia' 2023

Visit: Showroom: No 195, Wanduragala, Kurunegala, Sri Lanka, www.selyntextiles.com

6.6 Afghan women, refugees in India, have come together to create something new from the waste of the fast-fashion industry. Working together, they create beautiful dolls from scraps of leftover fabric with SilaiWali, a MADE51 partner.

MADE51

14 countries throughout Africa, Asia and the Middle East

FACTS

Founded: 2018

Founder: UNHCR, the UN Refugee Agency

Visit: www.made51.org

Launched in 2018, MADE51 is a trademarked global brand established by UNHCR (the United Nations' Refugee Agency, which protects rights for refugees, forcibly displaced communities and stateless people fleeing violence). The brand brings refugee-made artisanal products to global markets utilising a collaborative model, which strengthens refugee socioeconomic inclusion, connects with new partners, positively transforms perceptions about refugees and empowers refugees to earn an income using artisanal skills. UNHCR works alongside the World Fair Trade Organization to connect groups of refugees to experienced local social enterprise partners in refugee-hosting countries.

Over 85% of the 3,700-plus artisans working on MADE51 products are women, most of whom support multiple family members, who benefit from increased household income. For many of these women, artisanal work is a rare opportunity to earn income in a way that is compatible with family duties. Because artisanal work is relatively informal and can often be done from home and on a part-time basis, many women are able to fit it in alongside the domestic responsibilities they often carry. According to UNHCR, female refugee artisans often report using their income on basic household needs, children's education and healthcare for family members. Many cite their ability to bring home income as a source of empowerment within their families and communities.

For a product to meet MADE51 design criteria, it must be produced in Fair Trade conditions and reflect the heritage of the refugees who make it. Many of the products, including homewares and accessories, are made from locally sourced natural fibres or upcycled materials. There is an emphasis on ensuring products reach consumers with storytelling that highlights their providence, helping to show that refugees can be talented, positive contributors if given the opportunity. By bringing the cultural heritage and skills of refugees into product design, it encourages preservation of these intangible assets that are all-too-often under threat when populations are forcibly displaced.

6.7 Woven baskets produced in collaboration with MADE51 partner Indego Africa and made by Burundian refugees living in Mahama and Kigeme refugee camps in Rwanda. These items were crafted with sisal and hand-dyed sweetgrass woven using traditional coil and plaiting techniques. Their bold colour is inspired by Rwanda's landscape.

6.8 The GoodWeave certification label provides assurance that rug and home-textile products are made without child, forced or bonded labour. It also means the purchase supports programmes that educate children and improve working conditions for adults in producer communities.

GoodWeave

HQ in Washington, DC, USA, programmes in India, Nepal, Bangladesh and Pakistan

As we learn more about the forced labour[19] and child labour[20] discovered in some supply chains of the interior design industry, we depend more heavily on third-party assessments. While the exploitation problem is growing, manufacturers often aren't aware they have an issue upstream in their resource supply chains. Much of the exploitation takes place in hidden, subcontracted supply chains or even home-based working. These outsourced supply chains are opaque, constantly changing and beyond the Tier One factories that are normally audited by companies. Therefore, the problem remains largely invisible.

Transparency within whole supply chains is vital but also the ability to understand the information being given and consistency in its presentation. Third-party certifiers may assess some certifications, although the public does not have full disclosure. Certifications which include the welfare of people in varying degrees include the Forestry Stewardship Council (FSC®), OEKO TEX®, Made in Green, Global Organic Textile Standard (GOTS), GoodWeave, RUGMARK and Cradle to Cradle – where levels of detail vary from ensuring publicly available corporate ethics and fair labour statements for the whole company through to third-party assessment and accreditation.

GoodWeave is the leading institution working to stop child labour in global supply chains through a market-based system and holistic approach. The organisation's three decades of experience in carpet supply chains is now being transferred to other sectors, including home textiles and apparel. The non-profit was formed by children's rights activist and Nobel Peace Prize laureate Kailash Satyarthi.

Nearly one in ten children are working in the global economy and nearly half of them, 79 million, are in hazardous work.[21] Five countries are identified as having rug products made with child and/or forced labour and 10 countries are listed as having textile products made with child and/or forced labour.[22] Through partnerships with importers, retailers and interior designers globally, GoodWeave gains full access to supplier networks and production sites. Frequent audits and unannounced inspections are conducted at all tiers of the supply chain to ensure GoodWeave requirements are met. When victims are found, a series of rehabilitative services and interventions are provided to the child or worker experiencing abuse. GoodWeave also implements and supports a range of preventative programmes in producer communities. These include early years education and daycare centres, remedial education, programmes that ensure children are in school, as well as workers' rights, literacy and financial literacy training and health services for adult workers.

RUGMARK India has also been working in the same area of driving out child slavery from the carpet-making industry, ensuring children have a free formal education and medical care. RUGMARK has certified more than 10 million carpets exported from India.

FACTS

Founded: 1994

Founder: Kailash Satyarthi

Visit: www.goodweave.org/find-certified-products

6.9 Cushion made from 100% upcycled fabrics, including life jackets, from a series featuring positive words – messages from and for the refugee community.

Love Welcomes

multiple locations, including refugee camps

Love Welcomes is another important initiative providing artisan employment, skills and dignity to refugees, while utilising more than 4 tonnes of fabrics diverted from landfill, including life jackets used by families fleeing their homes by sea. The social enterprise, launched in response to the refugee crisis in Greece in 2017, has collaborated with Margo Selby and Joseph on designs for their handmade products, with more collaborations on the way. In every country where Love Welcomes works, it pays above that country's living wage, to assist financial independence and help support refugee women to rebuild their lives. The working week includes free life-skills training to adjust to language, finances and culture, along with medical supervision.

More than 100 million people have been forcibly displaced by war, violence, disturbing public order events and persecution.[23] The UNHCR estimates that it can take 15 to 25 years for refugees to become self-reliant.

The grim reality is that rising global boiling means climate vulnerability for huge amounts of the world's population, who will need to leave their homes. Climate refugees will far exceed the already disturbing current numbers of displaced people. The Ecological Threat Register produced by the Institute for Economics and Peace analyses risk from population growth, water stress, food insecurity, droughts, floods, cyclones, rising temperatures and sea levels. The analysis finds that the 19 peaceful countries which have the highest number of ecological threats have a combined population of 2.1 billion people, which is around 25% of the world's total population. A total of 141 countries will be exposed to at least one ecological threat by 2050. The institute estimates, 'In 2050, 3.4 billion people will reside in countries facing catastrophic ecological threats, compared to 2 billion in 2022. Their populations will account for 34.7% of the world's total population.'[24] This really brings into sharp focus the speed with which the world needs to reach net zero, which for many organisations and governments is currently 2050. It's not nearly fast enough.

FACTS

Founded: 2017

Founders: Abi Hewitt, the women of the Ritsona refugee camp and Becca Stevens

Visit: www.lovewelcomes.org

🔍 explore

Changing Streams, plastic use in the UK construction industry: www.changingstreams.org.

International Accord: www.internationalaccord.org.

Untold Creative, 'The True Cost', documentary film, 2016, www.truecostmovie.com

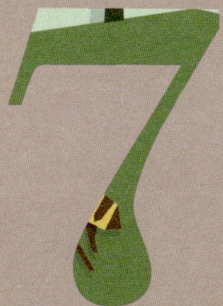

7

Place

'If you think about your home or your office building, they're routed to place, but unfortunately, that's where the comparison tends to end.

You see a flower has to get all of its energy from the sun through photosynthesis, it has to get all the water that it needs from the amount of precipitation that it can capture in the root system below. And it has to be adapted very specifically to a place that it can't pollute the soil and the earth around it, or it dies. In fact, when it's done that becomes nutrients for the next cycle. And while it's alive, it responds actively to temperature and humidity, it opens and closes and tracks the sun, and is actually habitat for lots of little critters, some that we see and some that we don't. And the kicker for me is that they're just so beautiful. Why can't this be a criteria for our buildings?'

Jason McLennan, CEO of the International Living Future Institute.

We can deeply connect to place in design by working with the surrounding topography, geography and cultural influences which enhance local identity, sense of familiarity, community and belonging. We can protect, restore and enhance the ecology of a place. We are connected to place by conserving the history left for us, and the history and knowledge we will leave to serve future generations.

There are insights and theories for how humans connect to and engage with our surroundings that we can utilise in design, such as psychogeography, which explores the body's emotional and be-havioural relationship to exploration of space and place, both natural and built. Architect Jo Petroni calls her permarchitecture method-ology of connection to place 'listening to your land'. To her, being curious, observing the natural elements, the history of the place, as well as connecting to the elders in the area helps grasp the essence of a place and leads to better designs. Ancient wisdom based around the five elements, either Vastu Shastra (a Sanskrit term meaning 'sci-ence of architecture') or feng shui (a Chinese term meaning 'the way of wind and water') – while not identical – bring wellbeing benefits to users based on the positioning of a building in relation to its the land, internal layout, views to nature and maximised daylight.

It is not a solely biophilic nature connection that humans have to place. A lack of a place identity results in placelessness – isolated spaces that are devoid of connection or emotional attachment, often used only for function and convenience. In contrast to this, my favourite community example from the book Happy City by Charles Montgomery is of two friends who were neighbours in Davis, California, who pulled down their fence to share gardens, and then went on to share meals and resources.[1] That was 1986: now N Street Cohousing is a thriving retrofit cohousing community model, as their 17 neighbours decided to also take down fences. Everyone still owns their house and garden. Residents each set their own preferences for visiting, borrowing and participating and can choose to be sociable or private when they want to be.

Vernacular materials and techniques bring a close relationship to the history and cultural identity of a place, while also preserving diminishing skills and crafts, resulting in more interaction and a deeper connection for those in the surrounding community. Using local materials and skills also tends to mean low embodied carbon and low transport mileage when sourcing, with manufacturing and storage all geographically close.

Barrio

Habitat, Byron Bay, Australia

The Australian Institute of Architects' award-winning Barrio neighbourhood restaurant sits within the Habitat, the mixed-use village project on the edge of Byron Bay's wetlands, completed in 2017. The whole neighbourhood is designed by Dominic Finlay Jones Architects, and is one where you can live, work and play, all in one place. The sense of place for this new development has been an important factor for how it has been embraced and accepted by the community.

The design of the village is based around landscaped gathering spaces rather than being car orientated. Pool cars and bikes can be shared, and there is even a solar-powered train connecting the area to the main part of town. Shop owners can live above their shops, so fewer commutes are needed and there is a healthier life/work balance. There are also workspaces – Dominic Finlay Jones has his studio on site. There is much needed accommodation for key workers, who are getting priced out of

7.1 Barrio restaurant – seating area.

7.2 Barrio restaurant – the outdoor seating area.

the area, as with many tourist destinations. The considered sense of community is created by thoughtfully locating shared spaces – shaded seating areas, community composting and growing, a pocket park, habitat for fauna and a lap pool, along with shops, fitness studios, salons and clinics to serve the community. Even the utilities serve to enhance the community. The site-generated solar energy is shared and greywater is treated through reed beds and reused in the village's toilets.

7.3 Barrio's rammed-earth bar sits within the pared-back material palette used for the interior, including the exposed construction shell, which needs no additions – just fixtures and lighting.

Open from daytime through to evening, Barrio is one of the eateries the new village is anchored around. The focus of creating the relaxed interior concept was on natural, simple and honest materials and detailing, and reduced use of materials. The centrepiece is the spectacular 25m-long bar, clad in rammed earth. Rammed earth is increasingly being revived and used for buildings in the area. This ancient method of compacting locally sourced earth, chalk, lime or gravel in a former (a mould) is sometimes stabilised with added cement, and is said to provide the strength of concrete without the high carbon footprint. It can be used for foundations, floors and walls, and here at Barrio, for the impressive bar made by local company Rammed Earth National. The clay used was sourced from the local Broken Head Quarry so reflects the earthy colours of the landscape within the restaurant's design scheme. There are generally two colour options for clay in this area, red or the yellow that has been used here. The composition works to regulate humidity, so improving air quality. The tactile finish has a long lifespan. The layered textural aesthetic needs nothing adding, just a countertop in PaperRock, a compressed recycled paper board, trimmed in local hardwood timber with integrated lighting.

FACTS

Clients: Tristain and Kassia Grier, Dan Wyllie and Francisco Smoje with Creative Capital

Architect and Interior design: DFJ Architects

Rammed-earth adviser: Rammed Earth National

Completion: 2017

Gross internal floor area: 270m²

Visit: Barrio, 1 Porter Street, Byron Bay NSW 2481, Australia, www.barriobyronbay.com.au

7.4 Barrio's impressive 25m-long rammed-earth bar.

7.5 A forest villa terrace. Tipai.

Tipai

Pandharkawada, India

❛ We weren't building a resort, we were sustaining a community.❜

Ariane Thakore Ginwala, designer[2]

The founder's aim for the creation of Tipai resort was 'extreme localisation'. Keyur Joshi had a long career in travel and wanted to break away from the standardised notion of what a luxurious wilderness retreat should be. He wanted this resort to give back by being regenerative, conserving the land and community it sat within, upskilling people, promoting the local culture, while sitting lightly on the land. The aims were to minimise concrete use, use local materials, build off the land, and apply all aspects of sustainability, including employing people from the local community and sharing skills with the community. This ethos runs through into the entire design brief and concept.

Working with designer Ariane Thakore Ginwala to create his whole vision, they soon found 35 acres of suitable land in central India, alongside the wilderness of Tipeshwar wildlife sanctuary. They both felt an instant connection to the land, a drought-prone zone and with a bare landscape in great need of restoration. Soil health had been depleted by teak farming practices, an issue in many parts of India leftover from British colonialism. Their intention was for the resort to follow permaculture principles to reach the goal of being self-sustaining in the coming years, growing food, living off the land, preserving water and generating electricity. They brought in a permaculturist to work out how to rejuvenate the land and wove this work in with the construction design and positioning. The permaculture landscaping was devised to rejuvenate the land using bio-massed trenches to enrich the soil, and the addition of natural vegetation, including the planting of 5,000 drought-tolerant native trees and low-maintenance plants such as bamboos and grasses to

support the existing ecosystem. Rainwater harvesting was a critical part of the plan, so each villa was built on top of a 75,000-litre tank to retain water on site. A seasonal stream runs through the site, and further water bodies were added, including a well and natural plunge pools with separate planted sections, with a natural filtration process using sand, gravel and plants, developed to be chemical free to avoid the use of chlorine.

The pair invested significant time in this exploration stage, investigating options for the construction of the resort around the natural landscape. The architecture evolved from their research and collaborations. Through researching local techniques, two hours away in Wardha they found the Centre of Science for Villages (CSV), which since the mid-1970s has been keeping rural building techniques alive and developing them. They began to collaborate with CSV and incorporated their learnings into the design. One of their techniques is a vaulted roof made from conical tiles. The shape is quick to build, flood- and earthquake-proof, uses local materials and is highly labour intensive, so generates employment. To waterproof the roof, broken tiles are used which also reflect sunlight to keep the interior cooler. The arch shape retains heat in the winter. Inside, the aesthetic effect is wonderful and as no further materials are needed, visitors see the beauty of the fired terracotta-clay interlocking cone shapes. This vaulted roof design is used for the pool residences. The forest villas, with verandas, have flat roofs using a hollow flat terracotta tile, again unfinished from inside, adding to the textural aesthetic alongside the other materials used.

Rammed-earth wall construction was an obvious solution to use alongside stonemasonry but proved problematic. With the help of a specialist who tested the local soil, it was found it would work if combined with a minimal amount of cement, so it met structural and waterproofing standards. The local community was trained and worked on building with conical tiles, forming rammed-earth and stone masonry, without the need for bringing in outside labour.

The interiors also evolved from local collaborations and are a celebration of Indian design and craft. Ginwala worked with lighting

7.6 A pool residence, with vaulted roof made from conical tiles developed by the Centre of Science for Villages; textiles were developed with the Magan Khadi Institute, including leaf-printed curtains.

7.7 A pool residence with terracotta-tiled roof, along with rammed-earth and stone walls.

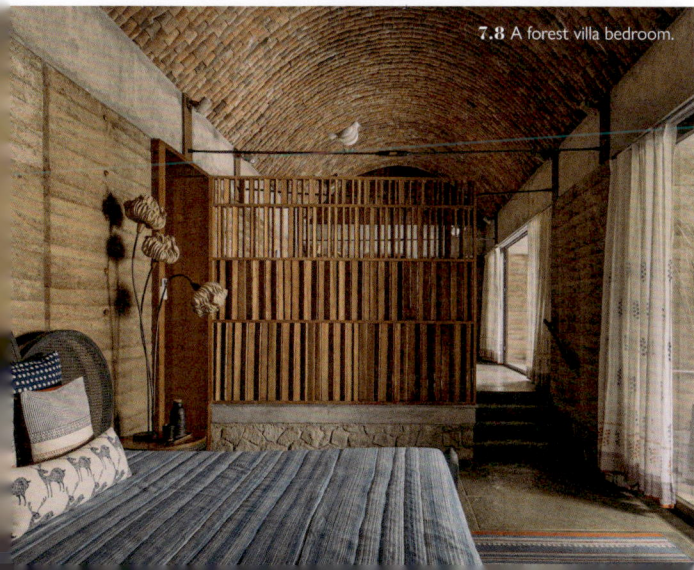

7.8 A forest villa bedroom.

7.9 Huge woven bird's-nest pendants and leaf-shaped wall lights in the main building.

designer Jenny Pinto of Oojaa Design on lighting, with shades made from banana fibre paper formed to replicate the local mahua flower shape, and with the craft design studio Wicker Story on woven, organic-shaped wall lights and dramatic large pendants for the main building. Terracotta floor tiles were sourced three hours away, with hardy patina which improves over time. Ceramic handbasins were handmade, as were rugs and the furniture; screens were made from reclaimed timber taken from Ginwala's own range for her contemporary craft furnishing company This And That.

Handwoven, naturally dyed 'khadi' textiles are used, made from locally farmed organic cotton. The textiles are made by the Magan Khadi Institute, which also resides in Wardha. Their fabrics are block printed, including using leaves as a printing block. Every piece of textile, from bedding and window coverage to cushions, upholstery, bathrobes and napkins, was made by the institute, from Ginwala and her team's designs.

The main 13.7m-high building houses one of the restaurants, and a bar, along with back-of-house maintenance, service housekeeping, a laundry and kitchen areas.

Ginwala has found this to be the most fulfilling project she has worked on. It's taken five years to build, with timeframes dictated by production times. Self-sufficiency is a few years away but in progress, with food being grown on site and a 100kW solar plant in place. The resort is a thriving biodiversity hotspot for flora and fauna, and home to more than 182 species of birds and animals, including the Bengal tiger. Roughly 100 people from the local community worked on the build, acquiring transferable new skills, and 80 people are now running the resort.

7.10 The resort's designer, Ariane Thakore Ginwala, with staff members at Tipai.

FACTS

Client: Keyur Joshi, Wildlife Luxuries

Spatial design: Ariane Thakore Ginwala

Rammed-earth adviser: Ata ur Raman

Permaculturist: Parag Mody

Structural engineer: Vinod Shah

Vaults construction lead: Centre of Science for Villages (CSV)

Completion: 2022

Gross internal floor area: 5,000m²

Visit: Resort (booking only), Pandharkawada, Gondwakadi, Maharashtra 445302, India, www.wildlifeluxuries.com

7.11 TECLA is the first dwelling built using two synchronised printer arms, using the Crane WASP 3D printer.

TECLA House prototype

Massa Lombarda, Italy

From nature's own building solutions, through observing how a potter wasp forms her nest, a collaboration between Mario Cucinella Architects and innovators in 3D printing World's Advanced Saving Project (WASP) formed to provide a fast, on-site solution to support crisis housing needs.

The project brings together research developed by the School of Sustainability, a professional school founded by Mario Cucinella Architects in 2015. It responds to the need for affordable housing for the growing global population, as well as for housing emergencies such as large migrations and natural disasters. The design for the home can adapt to multiple environments and is part of a masterplan of multiple self-sufficient homes, capable of producing, distributing or circulating water, energy and waste. The efficient design is reusable, recyclable and will biodegrade back into the land it was taken from.

The Crane WASP 3D printer is the world's first modular and multilevel printer able to build individual buildings. Using this same 3D printer, WASP had previously developed the Gaia house from mixing 25% site soil with 65% rice-production fibrous materials, combined with lime, to build a single space with an insulation cavity,

7.12 The pioneering TECLA dwelling – whose name and construction combine technology and clay – is formed using WASP's Crane 3D printer, using raw earth from the local terrain.

which is biodegradable if not maintained. The outer wall casing took just 10 days and €900 in materials to produce.

The design of the TECLA house uses the interlocking double-dome solution of ancient dwellings. The mono material creates the structure, roof, external cladding and the beautiful ribbed interior forms, without the need for any additional material. Ribbing thickness can be increased to suit thermal mass, and the cavity is insulated with rice husks. Humidity is regulated by the earth mixture. The interior space provides a living area with kitchen, bedroom and bathroom.

Each dome has an openable circular skylight for ventilation, with a circular LED light fitted below, and lighting is supplemented for day and night with concealed LED fittings inside and outside. Cable routes run in the integrated insulation cavity. The entire project is Italian made and uses natural, local materials. A continuous Terracruda® rammed-clay-based floor runs throughout and is

oil protected. This floor helps to regulate the indoor temperature, humidity, mould and acoustics.

Furniture is partly 3D printed, with the structure casing in the same local material. The seating is made from recycled cardboard by Officine Tamborrino. Orange Fiber's poplin fabric was used for bedding, made with fibre from recycled citrus juice by-products.

The TECLA house was printed in 200 hours using 60m³ of materials from the local terrain, set up by two people, using less than 6kW of energy, which equates to roughly 1.4 tonnes of carbon emissions.

Cucinella went on to experiment on a design for a 3D-printed TECLA chair for manufacturer Sawaya & Moroni, 3D-printed in recycled Plasmix, a combination of so-called dirty plastics – mixed post-consumer waste packaging diverted from landfill. The chair was exhibited at Salone del Mobile and is now in Sawaya & Moroni's range.

7.13 The ribbed interior of the TECLA house.

7.14 A TECLA chair, 3D-printed in Plasmix recycled plastic.

7.15 TECLA house – bathroom.

7.16 TECLA house – external view.

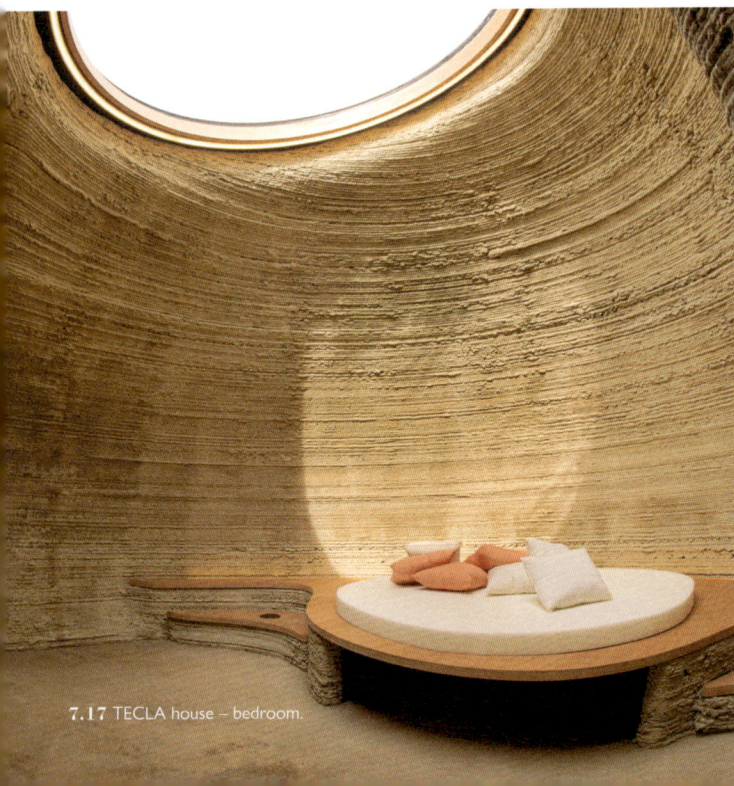
7.17 TECLA house – bedroom.

FACTS

Client: Municipality of Massa Lombarda

Architect and interior design: Mario Cucinella Architects and School of Sustainability

Engineering/3D-printing technology: WASP

Lighting designer: Lucifero's Lighting

Completion: 2020

Gross internal floor area: 60m²

Visit: www.mcarchitects.it/en/projects/tecla-technology-and-clay, www.sawayamoroni.com

StoneCycling® + Blended Materials

Netherlands

Site waste is a concern to many of us who work in the construction industry as we witness the industry's 50% contribution[3] to landfill first-hand. The team at StoneCycling®, led by Tom van Soest and Ward Massa, has been experimenting with reuse of high-value waste since van Soest's time at Eindhoven's Design Academy. It made steady progress, developing a tile-and-brick format and getting it through the necessary testing for health, safety and environmental legal requirements. The products attracted great press coverage and van Soest was awarded the Young Designer Award after exhibiting at Dutch Design Week in 2016. A production partner followed, and they began supplying their products to international projects, to be used on façades and in both commercial and residential interiors.

B-Corp-certified™ eyewear company Ace & Tate audits all its suppliers for impact on people and the planet using third-party auditors before working with them. The company's Barcelona store concept is inspired by Spain's first World Fair in 1888, showcasing modernity and industrial advances. Ace & Tate's in-house designers wanted to show unexpected materials in a modern and sleek way within their design. StoneCycling® and its products fitted the company's values and brief. Two colours of WasteBasedSlips® were used on lower wall sections: 'nougat sliced' and 'orange sliced'. The slip tiles were sliced partway through the production process to reveal the inside texture of the tiles and have a less raw finish. The project reused 900kg of site waste, recovered locally to StoneCycling®.

2G2W (too good to waste) WasteBasedBricks®, produced by StoneCycling® using pre-consumer production waste from its own factory, were specified by designers Quadrant4 for its client LC Packaging's new BREEAM 'Outstanding'-certified headquarters in Waddinxveen, the Netherlands. These bricks use 150kg of waste per m^2 of brick surface, diverting at total of 46,415kg of site waste from landfill.

All bricks and tiles come with an Environmental Product Declaration (EPD), along with a Life Cycle Analysis (LCA) for clarity and ease of comparison to support informed decision-making. Currently, all the highly durable products are made with at least 60% reused site waste, but StoneCycling® is working towards 100%. The team is developing a biodegradable plant-based tile for interior wall cladding. Aware that high-temperature coal- or gas-fired brick production emits large amounts of CO_2e, the team is reinventing this process with their production partner Zilverschoon Randwijk to switch to hydrogen-fuelled firing, making the process carbon neutral.

7.18 WasteBasedSlips® on the lower wall sections and around fixtures in the Barcelona branch of Ace & Tate.

Glazed versions of the WasteBasedSlips® with innovative waste-based glazing were used in the flagship Anne&Max café in Haarlem, in the Netherlands, by designers Studio JAAF, as part of its sustainable design concept, beautifully conveying their client's values to patrons. The tiles for the project upcycled 416kg (416m^2) of site waste.

While Ward Massa heads up the StoneCycling® developments, Tom van Soest, while still involved in StoneCycling®, has gone on to set up design studio Blended Materials to successfully develop glazed interior tiles made from 100% waste. With no use of scarce raw materials from nature needed, these tiles use regional waste collected up to 70km away. Clients are also offered a custom waste service where their own site waste is upcycled into tiles, diverting waste from landfill.

7.20 WasteBasedSlips® at the Anne&Max café in Haarlem.

FACTS

STONECYCLING®

Founded: 2014

Founders: Tom van Soest, Ward Massa

Visit: www.stonecycling.com

BLENDED MATERIALS

Founded: 2023

Founder: Tom van Soest

Visit: Showroom: Sint Jorisstraat 54, 5954 AP Beesel, Netherlands, www.blended-materials.com

explore

Jo Petroni, Permarchitecture e-book and course, www.permarchitecture.net

Colin Ellard, *Places of the Heart – The Psychogeography of Everyday Life*, Bellevue Literary Press, 2015.

Charles Montgomery, *Happy City – Transforming our Lives Through Urban Design*, Penguin Books, 2013.

N Street Cohousing, www.nstreetcohousing.org

7.21 Blended Materials tiles, handmade from 100% site waste.

8

Biophilic Design

'Treat nature as if your life depends on it. Recognise it does, then do something about it.'

Dr Sylvia Earle, President and Chairman of Mission Blue/The Sylvia Earle Alliance, National Geographic Society Explorer in Residence[1]

While there are many overlaps with healthy building principles, biophilic design is a unique approach. Biophilia is our love of nature and our connection to it. We are one of the 8.78 million species that share this home. We are interdependent with nature, as we are nature. Our understanding and appreciation of this vital relationship has recently boomed and subsequently biophilic design has a large following in the interior design industry, among people who recognise this necessary connection between humans and the health of the planet.

One major misconception about biophilic design is that it is solely about plants. As vitally important as plants are to the wellness of humans, our shared living system is very much more than that. Our planet is water based, with tides and gravity, and we are fuelled by the sun. Our precious soil has its own ecosystem. World-renowned biologist Edward O Wilson identified the term 'biophilia' as the connections that have evolved of humans and nature and the physiology which connects deeply to our senses, feelings and the instincts of humans through history. Stephen Kellert worked with Wilson on the theory and went on to develop it further and is often referred to as 'the father of biophilic design'.

Wilson and Kellert defined nature as light, air, water, plants, animals, weather, natural landscapes and ecosystems, and fire,[2] which connect to our senses through sounds, smells, the feeling of wind, sun and rain, colours, shapes, textures and patterns. Kellert summarised the connections between humans and nature in relation to spaces to include feelings of prospect and refuge, exploration and discovery, security and protection, fear and awe.[3] With this information we can design exterior and interior spaces that feed the senses and nourish human health while sitting lightly on the environment and being a part of it.

Stephen Kellert explained, 'Biophilic design is the deliberate attempt to translate an understanding of the inherent human affinity to affiliate with natural systems and processes – known as biophilia – into the design of the built environment.'[4]

How we live as part of nature is changing significantly. The urbanisation of humans has happened rapidly and relatively recently in our history. Significantly, in 2008 the planet's population shifted from the majority of the population living in urban environments rather than rural.[5] The term 'nature deficit disorder' is used to refer to this detachment.

We are losing our understanding and knowledge of nature, along with the lessons learnt from it, all proving to negatively impact human mental health. In the UK, the Woodland Trust surveyed 16- to 24-year-olds, finding seven out of ten young people are experiencing climate anxiety, but 86% felt that being outdoors in nature positively helped their mental health.[6] Since the early 1980s, shinrin-yoku (forest bathing) has been recommended by clinicians in Japan, and has been part of the country's national health programme. Forest bathing is an ancient Japanese process of relaxation, appreciating quiet among trees through all your senses. This recognition continues worldwide as time in nature is being prescribed more and more routinely by clinicians.[7]

These are two great examples on the effect of biophilia on humans that have stood out to me:

Natural light

Connection to daylight alone significantly improves psychological wellness. It activates our circadian rhythm, the body's biological rhythm and inner clock which regulates the body to prepare for and suit the time of day. By supporting the human body with the right amounts and colours of light, at the right times of day, we can radically improve wellness. In researching her book *Chasing the Sun*, science and medical journalist Linda Geddes lived the lives of gamblers in day-round artificially lit Las Vegas casinos, and the Amish, who shun the use of electric light and wake and sleep with the sun's cycles.[8] She and her family went on to experiment with brightening their days and dimming their evenings by eating and exercising outside, lunchtime walks, cycling and living by candlelight after dusk. While the weeks of the experiment took some adjustment, everyone felt the benefits of better sleep and mood. In particular, they were reluctant to revert to electric light in the evenings.[9]

Greenery

Green roofs can provide building insulation and cooling, capture water for greywater reuse (relieving the management of stormwater), integrate buildings into a landscape and reinstate farmland by transferring it onto the roof of the building. Green roofs can be coupled with tree planting to provide shade, remove heat from the air thorough transpiration, and reduce the effect of heat islands, where the temperature within urban areas is hotter than in rural ones. The addition of easily accessible greenery through pocket parks and even parklets (which take an area the size of a car parking space and replace it with planting beds and a place to sit) results in a significant benefit to humans and the local wildlife. In a Canadian scientific study, it was found that adding 10 trees to a city block in Toronto, increasing the tree density of the area by just 4%, benefitted residents in terms of improved health perception. It made them feel seven years younger and could be valued at what a $10,000 increase of income would mean in enabling them to move to a higher median income area.[10]

Urban food production provides an easy connection to nature for a building's users, who can learn skills about permaculture through growing food, seed swaps and also the growing of medicinal gardens and even the growing of plants for natural dyes in the case of the roof garden at New York's Fashion Institute of Technology building. There are many opportunities within the built environment to put nature back and reconnect us to growing through green roofs, rooftop farms, green walls and fruit trees. Where food growing happens, a community network of people follows.

Biophilic design brings benefits to different building types. In the healthcare sector, this was observed by Florence Nightingale in *Notes on Hospitals*,[11] published in 1863. In this book, she shared her extensive knowledge of hospital design, which included biophilic design principles in which nature promotes recovery, with bedheads positioned close to windows for reading by daylight and views to nature. In a slightly later letter to Edwin Chadwick[12] she records the benefits to patient recovery rates from bedroom ventilation and daytime open-air exercise. These findings were supported by Professor Roger S Ulrich in 1984. For more than nine years, surgical patients in a Pennsylvanian hospital were monitored for their recovery rates, comparing views to a natural scene including trees and a monotonous brick wall. Even though it was only a small positive difference, the results have gone on to influence hospital design since, as those with views of nature had shorter post-operative stays, made fewer complaints, took lighter doses of analgesics and had slightly fewer postsurgical complications.[13]

In UK workplaces, work-related stress, depression or anxiety account for 51% of absences (an average of 18.6 days of absence a year).[14] In a study, the favourable effects of viewing or spending time in green and blue space, such as rivers, canals and docks, were found to enhance employee mental health and cognitive ability.[15]

Studies on biophilic design used in education buildings show that more natural daylight means increased speed of learning (by around 20%), an improved attendance (averaging an additional three to four days a year), improved test scores (by 5 to 14%), improved creative thinking and reduced stress.[16] It is extremely disturbing, then, to learn that 45% of global office workers work with no daylight.[17]

Biophilic design assists our urban environments. The principles have been applied to cities, communities, homes, schools, universities, resorts, offices, healthcare, hospitality, railway stations, museums and fire stations.[18] Why wouldn't we design spaces that have so much restorative benefit to users, lowering blood pressure and stress levels, or enhancing immune systems, alertness, concentration, mood improvement, happiness and productivity?

8.1 The soothing and restorative Re:Mind studio space.

Re:Mind Studio

London, UK

British architectural and interior designer Oliver Heath, of Oliver Heath Design, and his team of spatial designers, researchers and experts in regenerative, biophilic, human-centred design have become international leaders in education on biophilic design. Their research is shared through the writing of a series of guides and books, and in practice through design for their clients' projects and products. Heath's Brighton-based practice thrives on initiating and implementing this research into diverse aspects of human-centred design. This covers a range of topics – from implementation of biophilic design for a range of financial budgets, enhancing connections to spaces and communities, inclusivity and the neurodiverse needs of users, to measuring impact and learning from analysis of pre- and post-occupancy evaluation to improve efficiencies and influence future designs. This evidence-based approach uses their valuable insights to make the design process more scientific and not about opinions. You could easily describe them as a research-based consultancy and strategists as much as a design studio.

The team were the perfect partners to help Re:Mind founder Yulia Kovaleva to deliver her vision of a studio to create a healing and calm environment for immersion in sound therapy, breathwork and energy healing; a space for stillness and quiet. It was quite a challenge to create such a nature-connected and peaceful space: the drop-in wellbeing centre is in Eccleston Yards in London's bustling and built-up Belgravia, complete with busy roads and underground trains nearby. Nevertheless, this studio needed to provide a restorative and human-centred experience for users through flexible and clever integration of the spaces.

In the studio space, a multisensory approach was adopted using aroma, sound and colour to deepen the natural connections and the experience of the space. The colour-therapy LED ceiling light bathes those meditating in the studio. The space is acoustically controlled for the comfort of users and detached from the busy city outside. Daylight is maximised for full circadian effect, and is controlled by roller blinds to soften the light.

8.2 Re:Mind founder Yulia Kovaleva.

The team's design provides a tranquil atmosphere, while also helping to improve health, wellbeing, productivity and creativity. Each end of the studio space has a focal point to frame the instructor. At one end, the lush green live plant wall in a ripple pattern is an attractive focal point, but also brings wellness benefits through seeing the organic forms, and filters toxins and CO_2 from the air. Non-toxic, natural materials, including reclaimed timber and clay paints, are used to reduce any chances of off-gassing during the studio's lifespan. A high-efficiency particulate air (HEPA) filtration system at floor and ceiling level is incorporated, which removes dust, pollen, mould, bacteria and any airborne particles that might be present or brought in from outside. Use of Douglas fir for floors and wall panels adds a distinct visual grain and soft warm natural hues, while providing a comforting warmth and texture to the touch. Cushions and mats for guests are organic cotton and linen, filled with organic buckwheat husks.

8.3 The multipurpose studio space in use.

8.4 Re:Mind's eco wellness store, selling plastic-free, natural products.

The tea area, with a combined boiling water filter tap and range of organic herbal teas, is designed to be a space of refuge, used flexibly and quietly. Finishes are textural and tactile, with deeply grained blackened timber base storage, glazed deep-pink handmade tiles, a recycled glass countertop, lush velvet seating, rustic stools and organic-shaped LED lighting.

This well-loved studio for 'finding your calm' is established as one of London's leading healing and community spaces. Quite an achievement for its size and location.

Danielle Brooker, of *Forbes* magazine, stated, 'It's easy to see why it's so popular – entering the space with the door reading "Find Your Calm", you are welcomed in with instant peacefulness, and encouraged to take the opportunity to create space for yourself both before and after your session.'[19]

At the opposite end of the studio space, the focal point is a Himalayan rock salt lamp light installation, within a circular opaque window which is shared with the adjoining space. While not proven, Himalayan rock salt lamps are said to attract pollutants, allergens and toxins and release negative ions to benefit health. Their soft, warm colours certainly add a gentle and restorative quality of light.

Plants, warm colour temperature lighting and pinkish colours, including the Douglas fir, are used throughout all spaces to promote restoration and relaxation. The reception flows into the eco wellness store and through to a relaxing tea area at the rear.

FACTS

Client: Yulia Kovaleva

Architect and interior design: Oliver Heath Design

Consulting mechanical engineers: Cundall

Completion: 2018

Gross internal floor area: 95m^2

Visit: Re:Mind Studio, 25A Eccleston Place, London SW1W 9NF, UK

Sharma Springs

Bali, Indonesia

'You can grow a house in four years.
And, in order to get there, in order to grow it,
you need sunlight, rain, water and not much
else... If you can build castles out of grass,
what else can you do?'

Elora Hardy, bamboo designer [20]

Naturally grown without any intervention once planted, bamboo, a giant wild grass, is little used. Bamboo designer Elora Hardy thinks, in addition, that it is not taken seriously. Bamboo is fast growing, as opposed to the several decades that timber takes, and it sequesters more carbon than some tree species and does this earlier in its lifetime. It is strong, with the tensile strength of steel and the compressive strength of concrete, and is traditionally used for building without the use of fossil fuels or emissions. Treated well, and properly prepared, installed and maintained, it will last for many decades. Japanese structures have historically lasted 200 years. The root system of a cut stalk will regrow. At the end of life, bamboo is regenerative with everything composting safely back to the earth.

Bamboo is an integral part of life for Balinese people. At birth, the umbilical cord is cut with sharpened bamboo. At death, bamboo is used to transport the body to the cemetery. A piece of yellow bamboo is placed in the left hand of the deceased to take to the afterlife to plant the bamboo for prosperity. Bamboo is not only important to biodiversity as habitat, but is also used for human habitat. Traditionally, untreated bamboo structures have had relatively short lifespans, despite being earthquake resistant. Hardy grew up in Bali, living there from the age of five months after her family moved from Canada, and they soon immersed themselves in Bali's culture. When they needed things, the family built them with bamboo.

Two decades later, Hardy's father, John Hardy, and his wife Cynthia created the Green School in Bali, a school with a nature-led curriculum promoting sustainable living and nurturing future changemakers. John Hardy had built a bamboo structure designed by architect Cheong Yew Kuan for his jewellery boutique. The pair were encouraged to also make the school campus in bamboo by their friend, interior designer Linda Garland, a pioneer and advocate of the use of bamboo. Garland had fallen in love with Bali when visiting in the 1970s and quickly recognised the importance of bamboo to life there. Bali became her home, and she began to integrate bamboo into her designs for the homes of her high-profile clients. She created the Environmental Bamboo Foundation (EBF), where ways of preserving bamboo were explored to take its use to a new level of both form and longevity.

At the time of the school's conception, Elora Hardy had visited her family from New York, where she had completed a Fine Arts degree and had been working for some years as a textile designer for Donna Karan, creating organic-form fabric designs. Hardy had read the book *Cradle to Cradle*,[21] which changed her life. She observed the disposable seasonality of fashion and was concerned about compromising the environment. Moving home to Bali, she asked to become involved in the Green School project, deepening her connection to nature and the craft of bamboo. She led the design team, and the Green School went on to be a winner of the Stephen R Kellert Biophilic Design Award.

Following completion, Hardy felt the deep desire to pay back Bali for her upbringing and experiences. The project had brought together the bamboo expertise of 120 artisans and architects for the creation and construction of the school and she felt a responsibility to them. The school had attracted families from all around the world, who wanted to live in environmentally friendly homes as well as giving their children a nature-based education. Hardy founded the architectural studio IBUKU to capture the gathered skills and continue Garland's advocacy for bamboo to build homes and structures. She and her team have continued to experiment with treatments to protect bamboo structures from insects and to develop techniques and push the boundaries for the

8.5 Sharma Springs – external view.

use of bamboo as a building material. The technical challenge for the Sharma Springs residence was to build it six storeys high, making it the tallest bamboo structure in Bali and pushing the boundaries for the conventional use of bamboo.

Consciousness of place psychogeography and psychology influenced the positioning of the building within the landscape. Balinese culture and tradition have a deep connection to nature and wellness, which is applied to architecture through using the five elements known as *pancamahabhut* – *pertiwi* (earth), *apah* (fluid), *teja* (light-energy), *bayu* (wind-air) and *akasa* (space) – which form all life between earth and sky. Set alongside the school's neighbouring Green Village, the house is positioned high on the forested cliffs on a ridge overlooking the windy Ayung River's valley.

The positioning meant a 9m drop to the land from the road, so the team designed a dramatic 'fear and awe'-evoking 15m-long tunnel bridge entrance where visitors land in the fourth floor open-air living, dining and kitchen spaces.

When problem-solving, the team's approach is to ask what nature would do and playfully replicate nature's shapes to form functions for the building. The three petal-shaped large roofs catch the breeze and provide the structure, along with a central tower with a winding helical staircase within. High ceilings capture the views and maximise daylight, while helping to keep the buildings cool with a natural convection current.

As with all the luxury homes IBUKU designs and constructs, Sharma Springs is almost entirely made from bamboo, and inside, some added wood, stone for countertops and hand-hammered brass used in bathrooms to protect shower walls. The team is well aware of the benefits of the shapes it uses, understanding the human stress response to sharp angles compared to how curves can increase cooperation and creativity.

8.6 Six storey high Sharma Springs residence

8.7 Sharma Springs – living area.

Many joyful and alternative solutions have been developed to solve problems, such as to hide appliances like the fridge-freezer, which sit in a woven pod. Doors are oval in a matching door opening, so feel more organic and playful. Bamboo is used to make doorknobs, light switches, furniture, even plumbing, all using forms taken from nature.

IBUKU created some enclosed rooms for the family, which are air conditioned, including the playroom, four bedrooms with en-suite bathrooms, and a library. Open areas have shutters at the windows to protect the interior from rainstorms. There's also an entry building, guest house, storage cave, wine cellar capped by a glass-floored pond, a riverside yoga pavilion, outdoor spa, plunge pool and a poolside barbecue, all surrounded by beautiful permaculture gardens.

Lush views to tropical forest and water make this a deeply biophilic experience for its users, enhanced by the thoughtful presence of biophilic design within the building.

Hardy demonstrates the importance and beauty of this exciting regenerative material by inspiring the building industry with her innovative approach: a joyful and elegant method while educating and pushing technological and regional boundaries for the use of bamboo. This evolution is a truly family affair. As well as the influence of IBUKU and the Green School, Hardy's brother Orin educates on bamboo architecture through Bamboo U. Linda Garland's son Arief Rabik continues her EBF work, promoting and sharing knowledge on bamboo as a sustainable complementary material to timber and assisting women in communities across Indonesia to farm bamboo to create an ecosystem and make a living while bringing back the forests that had been there in the past.

Neil Thomas, of structural engineers Atelier One, is also investigating the use of bamboo as a building material and has subsequently worked on award wining projects with IBUKU. He explains:

The human race has lost sight of its symbiotic relationship with the natural world. Biophilic design represents an attempt to redress this disconnect. For our own part, Atelier One is working to promote the use of natural materials and to exploit their potential in the urgent battle to address the challenges posed by climate change. As part of this mission, we have spent over a decade investigating the use of bamboo as a complementary material to timber. I firmly believe that, in my lifetime, bamboo will be an integral part of the palette of building materials favoured by the industrialised world.[22]

FACTS

Client: Sharma family

Architect and interior design: IBUKU

Construction: Bamboo Pure (a sister company to IBUKU)

Completion: 2013

Gross internal floor area: 750m²

Visit: Green Village, Jl Tanah Ayu, Sibang Gede, Abiansemal, Badung 80352, Bali, Indonesia

8.8 Bathroom with hand-hammered brass wall detail.

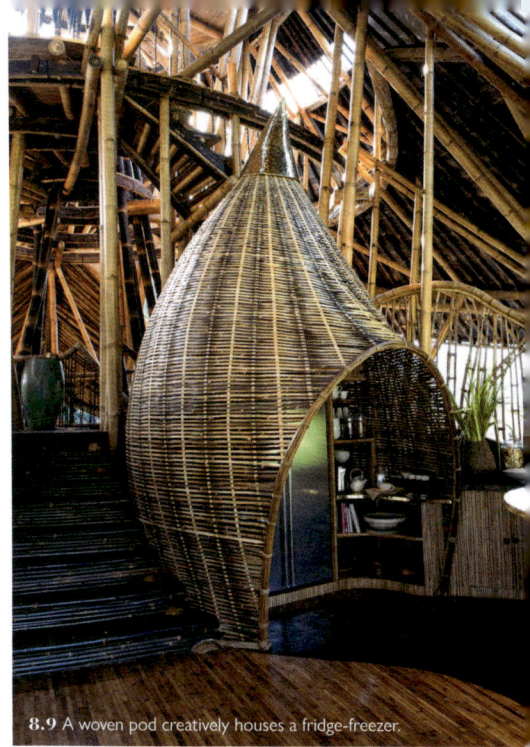
8.9 A woven pod creatively houses a fridge-freezer.

8.10 The oval shaped door set can be centre pivoted as well as the conventional side hinged.

8.11 A suspended bed, with bamboo shelving to the side.

Buffet Attraction
+ Terrace Apartment

Estudio Guto Requena, São Paulo, Brazil

Estudio Guto Requena's made-to-order Buffet Attraction sideboard combines algorithms with CNC machining for a biophilic effect with a beautiful organic ripple texture. This is one type of biomimicry – the copying of nature's forms and patterns which are found to nurture and calm us.

Alongside the design studio, architect Guto Requena created a research lab, Juntxs Lab, where parametric design is explored, creating shapes from algorithms. The contoured shape of the Buffet Attraction sideboard is created by digitally synthesising the energy force fields formed between attractors; these replicated shapes are carved into the three-dimensional form in high-tech precision by a CNC machine. The effect is further enhanced by the timber's natural grain.

In Brazil, timber must carry a full chain of custody. Nearly 50% of Brazil's forest is the Amazon rainforest, and 13% is the Atlantic Forest;[23] both are important hotspots for biodiversity. The Brazilian Forest Code was made law in 1965, updated in 2012 and is currently being strengthened to enforce protection of forests. The Amazon rainforest is made up of land from eight South American nations, who have pledged to end illegal deforestation of the Amazon rainforest by 2030.

The Buffet Attraction sideboard is produced in Tauari wood, a harder timber commonly known as Brazilian oak, and it comes with reforestation certification and chain of custody.

The sideboard was designed by the studio for Terrace Apartment, the home of creative director Guto Requena and his husband, in an

8.12 The Buffet Attraction sideboard in situ within Terrace Apartment.

8.13 Buffet Attraction sideboard, designed by Estudio Guto Requena.

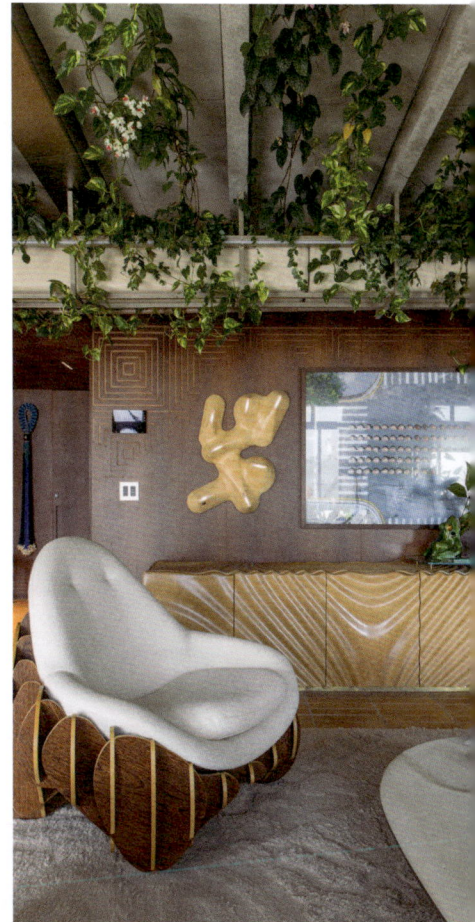

8.14 The Heart Wall installation, sitting on the wall above the Buffet Attraction sideboard, providing the apartment's heartbeat.

8.15 As the apartment had no terrace, the interior of the flat became the terrace, a space for growing plants and food, and maximising daylight.

8.16 Sliding walls and bookcases along with movable furniture means the space can be easily adapted to suit the use of the couple.

iconic Brutalist building in São Paulo, built in 1962. Buffet Attraction sits alongside a collection of vintage and contemporary Brazilian and international furniture and decoration. The apartment's design is the result of Requena's research over 20 years for his book *Hybrid Dwelling: Subjectivities and Home Architecture in The Digital Age*.[24] The book explores the impacts of technology and how being hyperconnected and highly technical impacts humans' way of living.

Technology is used throughout the apartment to enhance the experience and comfort of the space but is carefully concealed so it doesn't feel too futuristic, but warm and human-centred instead. Home automation is present for lighting, audio, video, window coverage, irrigation of plants and moving furniture, as the design of the apartment cleverly reconfigures to suit multiple functions, from working to a cinema set-up or a large open space for a party. The residents are treated to a lush indoor forest, fruit trees and a vegetable garden, along with furniture, finishes and artwork that are homages to Brazilian culture and design. Meanwhile the concealed technology controls daylight, temperature and sound comfort, and assists the usability and energy efficiency of the apartment. Another parametric design is the Heart Wall installation, in the form of a heart with seven individual LED lights, each synchronised to a heartbeat of a loved one, programmed by touching its BPM sensor.

Finishes and lighting have been carefully selected to support the liveable and sustainable brief. The old timber floor was removed and repurposed into furniture for the apartment. Brazilian-made terracotta-tile floors span most of the apartment; rugs designed in-house have been added in certain areas for comfort. The plant intensity used throughout the apartment has created a microclimate, reducing high temperatures and improving air quality. All factors combine to provide a highly desirable and liveable space.

FACTS

Architect and interior design: Guto Requena and Estudio Guto Requena

Lighting designer: Foco Luz e Desenho

Completion: 2022

Gross internal floor area: 280m²

Visit: www.gutorequena.com/buffetatracao

explore

Stephen R Kellert, *Nature by Design: The Practice of Biophilic Design*, Yale University Press, 2018.

Stephen R Kellert and Edward O Wilson, T*he Biophilia Hypothesis*, Island Press, 1993.

Living Building Challenge®:

   Biophilic Design Toolkit, www2.living-future.org/biophilicdesigntoolkit

   Stephen R Kellert Biophilic Design Award

Oliver Heath Design guides: www.oliverheath.com/consultancy-and-research/whitepapers

Elora Hardy:

   'Magical houses, made of bamboo', TED2015, 19 May 2015.

   'Bali: Sharma Springs', series 1, episode 3 of 'Home', Apple TV +, 17 April 2020.

Guto Requena, *Hybrid Dwelling: Subjectivities and Home Architecture in the Digital Age*, Senac SP, 2019.

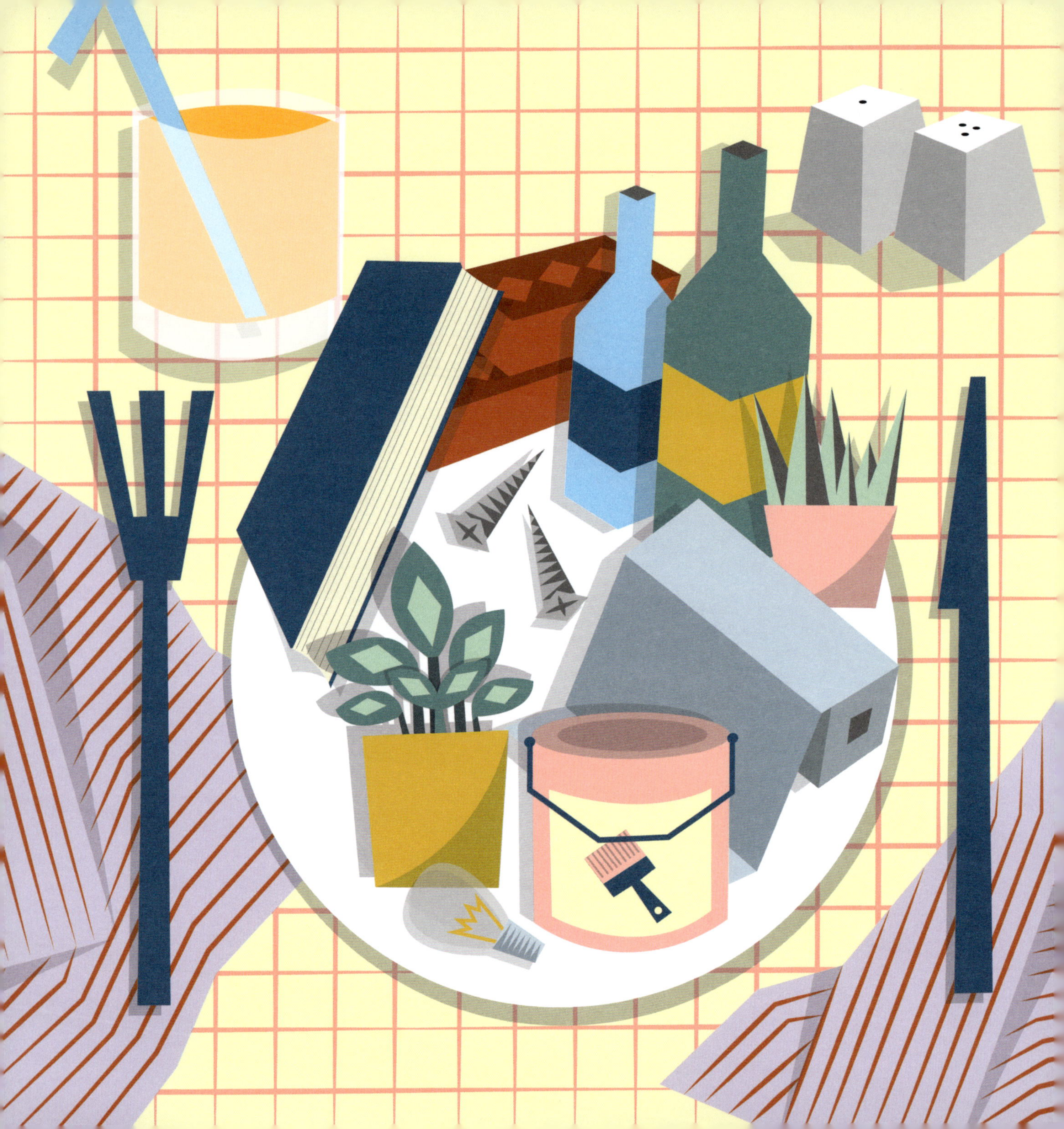

9

Healthy Building

'We are where we live as much as we are what we eat.'

Alison Mears, Associate Professor of Architecture, Director and Cofounder, Parsons Healthy Materials Lab[1]

Good design surely has to be centred around people, doesn't it? For so long, design has been about beauty, ergonomics, accessibility, safety and experiences, but it is surprising that it's really only relatively recently that the multiple facets of healthy building have started to come into the interior designer's scope as the Healthy Building Movement has come to the forefront of the construction industry. Methods like building biology and biophilic design, and third-party certifications WELL Building Standard, Fitwel and the Living Building Challenge®, address the function of buildings to support the health of occupants, even encouraging activity and wellness within them.

A human-centred design approach addresses the many ways a building can affect its users' health and ensures they are positive. Buildings are an opportunity to encourage better health through both how they are formed and what we put inside them. While some of the theory is based on biophilic design through how nature affects us, the approach also involves the biology of a building, both its construction and fabric, as well as how it breathes and is maintained.

There are so many ways an interior can negatively impact its users. For some decades we have been aware of 'sick building syndrome' being the effects of poor lighting, ventilation and air quality, layouts and cleaning on building users.[2] More recently, as buildings are designed to be more and more airtight and energy efficient, we find ourselves increasingly trapped inside with materials that can harm us. The German Environment Agency has identified that the use of chemicals is steadily increasing globally.[3] Outside, airborne pollution is a major contributor to deaths each year. Look up the statistics for where you are. Around 170 deaths on average are recorded a year in my hometown of Brighton and Hove, UK.[4] Shockingly, indoor pollutant air levels may be two to ten times higher than outdoor

levels.[5] Therefore, indoor air quality has been increasingly important to monitor, summarised as the '3Ps':

pathogens and microbes – organisms that are brought in from outside or grown inside

pollution – from gas cooking, wood burners, cigarette smoke, particulates brought in from outside, radon

products added to a building – finishes, furniture, fittings and equipment (FF&E), personal care products and cleaning chemicals. The sources of off-gassing are volatile organic compounds (VOCs) released from furniture, paints and finishes, additives (phthalates, formaldehyde, flame-retardancy chemicals), PFAS ('forever chemicals', which can be found in fabrics, paints, flooring, coatings, lacquers, grout, caulk, adhesives[6]) and ozone (released from printers).

A group of researchers in US universities had discovered that dust samples collected in university rooms were hormonally active. They went on to carry out a more detailed study where indoor air quality was tested in a study of people working in offices in the UK, US, India and China. Workers each wore a silicon wristband for a week during their work shifts that collected chemicals in the air. When the wristbands were examined, the researchers discovered that every worker had been exposed to a cocktail of hormone-disrupting chemicals, including plasticisers, fragrance, flame retardants and pesticides. The women monitored were found to be exposed to a greater number of chemicals, possibly due to these chemicals being used in personal care products.[7]

Toxic chemicals are even making their way into our pets' bodies, as found by US biophysical chemist Arlene Blume when her cat was examined after developing hyperthyroid disease: flame-retardant chemicals (PBDEs) are believed to have migrated out of furniture and accumulated in house dust, which her cat had ingested. Blume went on to cofound the Green Science Policy Institute (GSPI) to protect human health and the environment from toxic chemicals used in everyday products by changing government policy in the US. As so many chemicals are used in industry, the institute grouped the chemicals of concern into Six Classes to ease understanding and to tackle the 80,000 chemicals used in the US. Alongside the Six Classes approach, the GSPI formed a materials buyers' club for like-minded businesses to group together to buy safer materials for their workplaces and encourage change in the supply chain. In addition to off-gassing, these chemicals find their way into our bodies through inhalation, ingestion and dermal absorption, and into the environment, water sources and food chains through degradation, leaching, abrasion and oxidation.

We need manufacturers to disclose ingredients so we can evaluate material health. The Living Building Challenge® has a regularly updated Red List[8] of 'worst in class' ingredients to avoid. These include formaldehyde, bisphenol-A, lead, mercury and PVC. Designers can simply ask suppliers if products are Red List Free. However, standardised sets of comparable information are also vital in making informed decisions. We are used to using Environmental Product Declarations (EPD) as a standardised way of evaluating environmental impact across a product's life cycle. The two main ways for manufacturers to voluntarily evaluate products for material health are Health Product Declarations® (HPD) and the Declare label from the International Living Future Institute (ILFI), who are behind the Living Building Challenge®. Both methods can be either third-party verified, or self-disclosed using software tools such as Toxnot, and stored on publicly accessible databases. Both require manufacturers to disclose ingredients present from 100ppm (0.01%) by weight. The Declare label highlights if Red List worst-in-class ingredients are present or if it is Red List Free. The label also discloses additional useful manufacturing information for evaluation, such as manufacturing locations, life expectancy, embodied carbon, end-of-life options and responsible sourcing, including Forestry Stewardship Council (FSC®) chain of custody.

Air ventilation and filtering can remove indoor pollutants. Regulating indoor humidity is vital to prevent mould; this can be done

mechanically or passively through the use of materials like clay plaster which can help to moderate humidity. Simply air-flushing a space twice a day can improve concentration, mood, blood pressure and heart rate. Careful design of entryways with self-closing doors and large entrance matting can prevent particulates from being transferred into the building.

Interior design can encourage occupants to make healthier, more active choices in buildings in so many ways, for example by providing nudges through the wide offering of healthy food choices available and easy access to filtered drinking water or encouraging the use of wearable technology to monitor and encourage movement and healthy sleep. An interior can boost activity inside via the provision of sit/stand work areas, active workstations with treadmills and bikes, and attractively designed staircases placed centrally to encourage use in place of lifts. There might be areas for exercise and yoga, and ease of access to exercise equipment, and restorative spaces such as vegetable patches or rest and mediation areas.

During the Covid-19 pandemic, the Healthy Building Movement came into its own. Employers have used the concepts to look after employees both in and outside of the workplace. The principles for filtering and handling of indoor air and cleaning routines have supported the management of the coronavirus, as well as the mental health support for the less visible repercussions of the virus on the wellbeing of employees.

Client Yvette Leeper-Bueno sitting outside Vinatería.

Vinateria

Harlem, New York City, USA

Jonsara Ruth is a well-respected educator and leader within the Healthy Building Movement. She's also a designer and artist. She founded and leads the design collective Salty Labs, based in Brooklyn, which delivers elevated human experiences, specialising in healthy materials that promote everyday human health and care for environmental health. She's cofounder and design director of the Healthy Materials Lab, a design research lab at Parsons School of Design in New York City. I discovered her through taking their Healthier Materials and Sustainable Building four-part online course.

The Vinateria restaurant project demonstrates the perfect combination of using healthier materials, avoiding materials with harmful ingredients, building with a lighter impact through avoiding virgin sources, using reused elements and so-called 'waste' materials, while not sacrificing or compromising the aesthetics and performance of the spaces that are created. The restaurant design represents the Parsons Healthy Materials Lab course perfectly.

Ruth's client, Yvette Leeper-Bueno, grew up in the Harlem community, an area which has recently experienced growing gentrification. Her client had not owned a restaurant before but wanted to create a meeting point in the form of a wine bar. The goal was to create a meeting place that would feel welcoming to both existing and new communities. Ruth didn't want it to look brand new or ostentatious and gentrified, so her team at Salty Labs experimented with materials and ideas as part of their collective's ethos. While it wasn't in her brief, Leeper-Bueno supported this, but it was vital the aesthetics had to be beautiful and appealing to her customers as well. The project began with searching for the right building, and a perfect corner site with large windows was found in Harlem.

The philosophy was to use as much of what was already on site as possible but make it new through design, an example being the existing external aluminium-framed glazed doors which were secure

and functioned perfectly well. Ruth collaborated with artist James Scott and they had his drawings laser cut into sheet aluminium panels to cover the glass, which casts patterned light around the interior.

The design team set about sourcing the right vintage furniture and fixtures, and beauty and nostalgia was important, such as the 1940s timber bar and backbar. The team brought in the expert services of lifelong collector Fritz Karch to source the remaining elements.

Vintage furniture, vessels and reclaimed fittings sourced by Karch proved to be better in quality than new, such as milk glass pendant lamps, glassware displays, aluminium food service ware, rescued café chairs, even vintage cutlery. Quirky design details were added throughout, such as the skirting-height coloured leg sections of the reclaimed bentwood chairs. Furniture was refinished in non-toxic, healthier finishes. The odd chair was not refinished to show old

9.2 Vinateria's front doors – existing aluminium-frame doors with replaced vintage door handles and inset aluminium panels laser cut with artwork by James Scott.

9.3 Vinateria bar area, with its dark-grey lime-plaster wall, repurposed 1940s bar, new zinc top, used stools and vintage factory lamps.

9.4 Vinateria bar area – white lime plaster is the backdrop to glass shelves with vintage glass barware.

alongside new. The occasional black unglazed porcelain floor tile was swapped with a white version. The team found craftspeople who appreciated their approach to collaborate with them on their alternative ideas.

The concept evolved beautifully during the project, as Ruth and the team skilfully negotiated the client's brief and budget. They were fortunate to be able to design areas as they went, sprinkled with lots of creativity and conscious material and finishes choices along the way.

Healthier material choices were made throughout. While the client had not asked for healthier materials in her brief and was unaware of any issues, it was something Ruth had raised and discussed, using the analogy of healthy food to describe the approach. Indoor air quality is moderated by the plaster used throughout – humidity, toxics and odour are continually absorbed into the wall surfaces. The lime plaster was painted with 'wall tattoo' fresco artwork applied in precise locations throughout the space. To avoid any off-gassing within the interior, inert materials were selected: stone, glass, unglazed porcelain floor tiles, reused and recycled metals.

For sound comfort, acoustics were softened with full-height wall sections made from panels of perforated wool felt, left over and salvaged from felt washer production.

The window planters are filled with herbs in the sunny dual-aspect windows. They look attractive from the outside, sitting within the black exterior, and also inside, where they emit their appetising scent.

Ruth finds the approach of using healthy and reused materials, while working collaboratively with craftspeople, is so much more creative and provides a more compelling experience which uplifts people's lives. Her description of herself as an 'agitator for design and a catalyst for healthy materials' fits her so well.

The client feels the restaurant's success is partly due to the food and partly due to the space. Ruth puts this down to the material choices. The client has enjoyed repeating the storytelling aspects of the design to her customers. This classic and timeless design has served her well and remains unchanged, except for the addition

9.5 The acoustic wall is made from waste wool felt; on the dark-grey far wall is a wall tattoo by artist Helen Quinn.

9.6 Vinateria dining room – church pews were remodelled to fit in the front corner; the table bases have custom zinc tops, and there are vintage milk glass lamp shades, unglazed porcelain floor tiles, lime paint on the walls and ceiling, and custom planters for rosemary and lavender plants.

9.7 The later addition of an outside dining structure alongside the restaurant.

of an outside dining area structure which Salty Labs later designed for her. Ruth stresses how hard business is in Manhattan, reporting that 80 to 85% of restaurants last only two years. This restaurant's classic design has already served it well for over 10 years and will serve it for many more. The alternative collaborative approach used by its creators seems to be one of the main reasons why.

FACTS

Client: Yvette Leeper-Bueno

Architect: BriggsKnowles Architects

Interior design: Salty Labs design collective; collaborators included Jonsara Ruth, Catherine Murphy, Fritz Karch, Livia Di Mario, Helen Quinn, James Scott, Gosia Rodek

Graphic designer: Livia Di Mario + Paolo Agostinelli

Completion: 2013

Gross internal floor area: 390m²

Visit: 2211 Frederick Douglass Boulevard, Harlem, NY 10026, USA, www.vinaterianyc.com

The Village Nursery

Bellingdon, Buckinghamshire, UK

Set in the Chiltern Hills is an unusual and beautiful nursery school constructed from healthy, local materials to support and nurture its early years users to learn and thrive. The project was a collaboration between earth architect Gernot Minke, hemp expert Will Stanwix and the client, brickmaker and builder HG Matthews Ltd, for the community surrounding the brickworks.

Minke's earthquake-resistant domes have been built worldwide as public buildings, schools, meditation spaces and community buildings. Jim Matthews, grandson of HG Matthews Ltd's founder, had seen a previous nursery school of Minke's with a dome, and so contacted him. This version for the Bellingdon village community was formed from a central dome with archways to the surrounding rooms around the outside forming an octagon, meaning children can see into all the rooms from the central dome and out to the surrounding gardens.

The main focus of the project for Will Stanwix and the HG Matthews team was to develop and test the local vernacular version of structural earth-block 'strocks' using clay and straw waste from the brickworks. The recyclable strocks are dried instead of fired so have very low embodied carbon. The team developed a version of the strock design to form the dome structure, leaving the beautiful internal face uncovered.

The materials, neutral colours and forms used provide a peaceful and calming experience, which is especially helpful for autistic children attending the nursery.

The indoor climate, the humidity and air quality are balanced and regulated passively without any mechanical ventilation system needed due to the hempcrete, made from hemp and lime, which insulates the walls and floor, and the clay and straw plaster used in the perimeter spaces. As designer and television presenter Kevin McCloud says, solutions that are 'old tech, low tech, high tech'.[9]

9.8 The structural earth-block 'strock' domes form the walls and ceiling. Children can easily view other spaces through the doorways.

9.9 The beautiful central earth-block dome of the octagonal building – the first of its type in the UK.

9.10 The octagonal nursery building has an insulating green wildflower roof which blends with the surrounding gardens where the children play and learn to grow plants.

Floors made from local oak are installed throughout. Underfloor heating via air source heat pump is installed but little additional heat is needed and the heating is only used a few times a year. HG Matthews made bespoke ceramic tiles for the kitchen and bathrooms and also decorative mosaics depicting nature, used in the perimeter rooms and entrance.

Flint rubble collected from local fields formed the trench foundations to avoid the use of concrete. Traditional handmade brick forms the exterior skin. These bricks are dried with biomass boilers and then wood-fired using local sustainable timber.

HG Matthews holds open days to share knowledge about the building and its construction. The nursery is loved by the community and is used by children from five months to eleven years old, from a five-mile radius. With a waiting list of children who aren't even born yet, this building will serve many future generations.

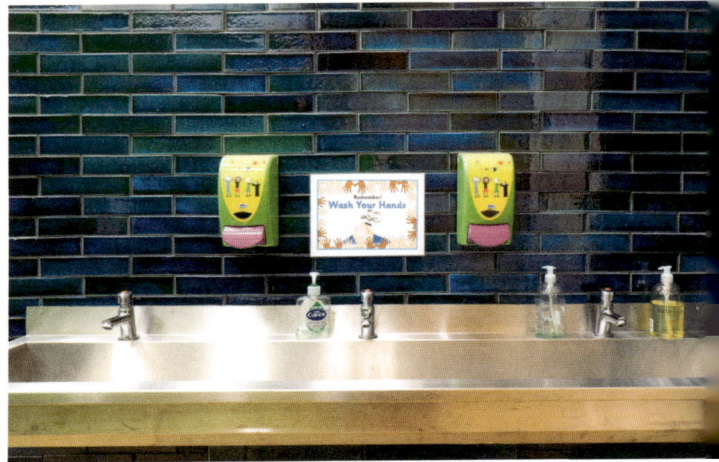

9.11 The bespoke ceramic tiles in the bathrooms.

FACTS

Client: HG Matthews Ltd

Architect: Gernot Minke

Lead construction coordinator: Will Stanwix

Completion: 2020

Gross internal floor area: 300m²

Path Chair

New York City, USA

For most of its products, New York-based furniture design and manufacturer Humanscale had used two voluntarily evaluation methods to self-identify any ingredients with health hazards and disclose the findings in a standardised way for comparison. These were the Health Product Declaration (HPD) and the Declare transparency nutrition label.

With the goal of producing the world's most sustainable task chair, the Path Chair, Humanscale chose to push further and pursue the Living Building Challenge® 'Living Product Challenge™' certification (LPC) for the chair rather than a HPD or Declare label. In doing this, Humanscale is industry-leading in its commitment to the transparency of its products and production. It means both the chair and the production operations have been third-party certified as being climate positive, energy positive, water positive and toxin free.

Going beyond 'doing less harm' or carbon neutral, the LPC certification means rather than having any negative-impact footprint – or no impact/neutral – the chair has a positive impact, referred to by the Living Building Challenge® as its 'handprint'.

This is quite a thing to achieve when not just the manufacturing process is assessed but the whole life cycle, from resource extraction of raw materials to manufacturing, transport, the use phase, through to end-of-life disposal. This has meant significant upgrading of the company's global manufacturing facilities and examining its processes. Reduction of water needed in production has been addressed, which conserves energy as well. Rainwater is captured on site and meets almost all the manufacturing-process water needs, including site irrigation. Through schemes, most of the production waste is diverted from landfill. However, none of this will shrink impact enough to have a zero footprint. It is unachievable without the 'handprinting' element, measurable new improvements such as influencing improvements for the supply chain and for workers, assisting projects in the community to help them conserve water and energy, and supporting biodiversity habitats and tree planting.

Bob King, founder and CEO of Humanscale, explained:

'You have to do what's not convenient. You have to work with not just your suppliers but their suppliers and sometimes their suppliers to get them to do the right thing. The great thing about that is now they can supply all their customers.

By doing this process you make this technology available to the whole industry. And that's one of the ways we get the industry to do what's right.'[10]

In achieving the materials health required for the chair's LPC optimal score, this task chair builds on previous heathier material advances and chemical replacements made for products by the company, such as eliminating the use of hexavalent chromium (chrome 6). Humanscale has removed all the worst-in-class ingredients harmful to humans and the environment, making the chair Red List Free. Material data is audited using software platform Toxnot.

Designed by industrial designer Todd Bracher, Humanscale's creative director, the material composition for the chair is a total

9.12 Humanscale Path Chair.

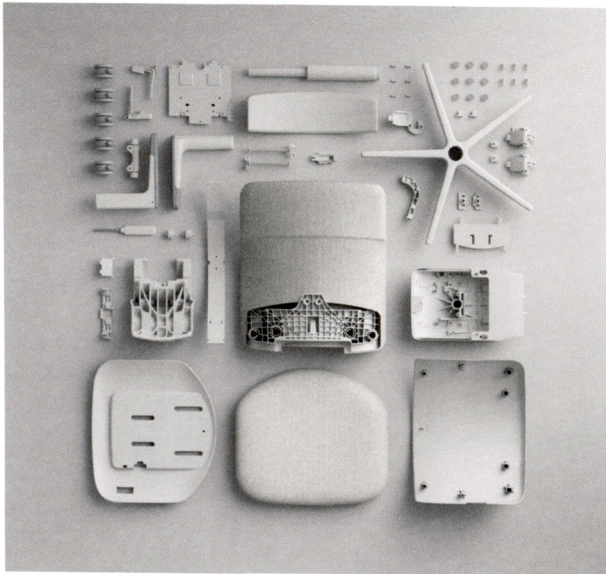

9.13 The design of the Path Chair has been simplified to use fewer components, making it easier to repair with available spare parts and easier to disassemble at end of life.

of 50% is recycled, including retrieved ocean plastic and post-consumer packaging waste plastic, including textiles developed with Kvadrat, and uses recycled aluminium content which needs far less energy to produce. Designed for its whole life cycle, it is easily repaired and disassembled. The design itself promotes health through user comfort. Rather than the industry norm of being designed to fit the 50th-percentile average-adult human size, the Path Chair is inclusively designed to fit 95% of the population's height, weight and width. Its gravity mechanism adapts to fit the user, so doesn't need fussy controls for adjusting or a training session to use, leaving the aesthetics of its shape minimal and uncluttered.

Following the development and manufacture of the Path Chair, Humanscale has impressively gone on to certify its whole range as meeting the Living Product Challenge™.

FACTS

Humanscale

Founded: 1983

Founder: Bob King

Awards (Path Chair): 2022 SEAL Sustainability Product Award; 2022 Metropolis Likes NYCxDesign Award; 2022 iF Design Award

Certifications: Living Product Challenge™

Visit: www.humanscale.com

explore

Green Science Policy Institute, Six Classes webinar series, www.sixclasses.org

Healthy Materials Lab: course, podcast, webinars

Healthier Materials and Sustainable Building, self-paced online four-part course.

Healthy Materials Lab: Trace Material podcast – series: hemp, plastic and mycelium.

HPD Public Repository: www.hpd-collaborative.org/streamline-green-building-product-selection

International Living Future Institute's Red List: www.living-future.org/red-list

Living Product Challenge™ and Declare label product database: www.declare.living-future.org

Mindful materials platform: www.mindfulmaterials.com

10

Climate and Biodiversity Emergency

❛We are in terrible, terrible trouble and the longer we wait to do something about it [rebalancing our natural world systems], the worse it is going to get. So the urgency with which we're dealing with it could not be exaggerated.

It is extremely urgent. We have time now, perhaps 10 years, perhaps 20 years, to do something about it. But the longer we leave it, the more difficult it will be to do something about it.

And if we leave it too long we won't be able to do something about it. And the natural systems with which we have grown , and the world has become populated, will collapse ❜

Sir David Attenborough, speaking at the International Monetary Fund spring meeting April 2019, Washington, DC.[1]

Biodiversity is all life on the planet. It is far from a nice-to-have, it is vital. For human life it is essential to protect biodiversity, as it is essential to our health and wellbeing, culture and the global economy.

Biodiversity provides essential services, freely, supporting our survival, and we cannot operate without it. Nature's land and aquatic ecosystems do so much that is essential to all life, such as protecting life within the biosphere and sequestering carbon. Not only is there increasing demand on food production as the human population grows, but pollinator insects are in decline, making our food systems unstable and affecting low-income countries more harshly due to the crop types that are impacted.[2]

One of the multiple threats to pollinator insects is habitat loss. Climate change is leading to biodiversity habitat and ecosystem loss through drought, storms, sea level rise, heatwaves and wildfires. We know from Rachel Carson's findings the impact that artificial pesticides used in modern farming have on birdlife.[3] In Europe, since 1980, we have lost over half a billion birds, with fossil-fuel derived pesticides and fertilisers being found to be the biggest cause.[4] The WWF's Living Planet Index has been tracking the trends in wildlife since 1970 and has found we have an average global loss of 69% of the planet's wildlife population, with freshwater species populations worst effected, with an 83% global decline.[5]

Continuously since 1958, with the exception of a volcanic eruption that damaged power lines, the Mauna Loa Observatory in Hawaii has been the benchmark sampling site for monitoring and collecting data related to global climate change, atmospheric composition and air quality. The observatory is best known for its measurements of rising anthropogenic greenhouse gases (GHG) in the atmosphere, commonly referred to as carbon dioxide (CO_2) or more correctly as CO_2 equivalent (CO_2e). The observatory holds the world's longest record of CO_2e monitoring and the levels are steadily rising.[6]

Nature's ability to regulate emissions of GHG is being undermined by the destruction of ecosystems. It's easy to see how the two emergencies are one and need to be urgently tackled together. Our natural systems need protection from collapse as they are interdependent. We need to save life on the planet and recognise the vital interconnection and interdependency of that life.

Where does the interior design industry fit in addressing the twin crises of climate change and biodiversity loss? Globally, buildings account for almost 39% of energy-related CO_2e emissions, of which 28% is operational carbon use to power, heat and cool them and 11% is embodied carbon in the materials used to create them.[7] Interior designers can make informed decisions about processes and material use, and influence decision-making within project teams. We can be creative with a limited palette. We can stop using fossil fuels and plastics and make low-impact choices for designs and specifications, addressing emissions, pollution, energy use and resource depletion so they are regenerative and self-sustaining. We can address lifespan, life cycles and waste. We can be advocates for people and animals, and address the impacts on them that our work has. We can collaborate and join forces for sharing knowledge and influencing change.

The Declare movement has grown where scientists, businesses and industries each formally declare that the climate and biodiversity emergencies exist. Sectors join and collaborate to address the issues, share learnings and influence policy to decarbonise and move away from the use of fossil fuels. Within the built environment, this started with Architects Declare in 2019, which led to international versions, and other sectors under the umbrella of Built Environment Declares, including Interior Design Declares, which I encourage all to join or help to set up if one doesn't yet exist in a country.

Local governments and even whole countries have also made declarations. Wales was the first country globally to declare a Climate Emergency in 2019. The Welsh Government had already introduced the revolutionary Wellbeing of Future Generations (Wales) Act 2015, a world-leading law led by Jane Davidson to improve the environment, economy, society and culture – all indicators of national wellbeing for both the current and future people of the country. This pioneering law to prioritise wellbeing over gross domestic product (GDP) is being replicated by the United Nations, Scotland, Finland, New Zealand, Iceland and Canada.

The Welsh Government even has a commissioner representing unborn generations. The Welsh Government's net-zero strategy, Wales Net Zero 2035, is embedded into public bodies and communities across Wales with a series of reduction challenges to minimise environmental impact and reduce climate vulnerability. The strategic plan includes suspending new road building in favour of subsidising public transport, a home insulation programme, solar photovoltaic panels for schools and public buildings, and community-owned renewable energy. The country has pledged to stop production of licensed oil and gas. All very inspiring for the small nation once dependant on the industries of steel, coal and iron.

One Planet modular home concept

Llandeilo, Wales

With the aspiration to become a One Planet Nation – one that is self-sustaining within a generation – the Welsh Government introduced One Planet Development (OPD). This ambitious and important planning policy is a template for living within our ecological footprint.

A measurement of 'global hectares' (gha) is used, which, along with carbon footprint, includes other aspects of resource consumption and how fast the Earth can replenish those resources. In Wales, this ecological footprint is the 14th National Wellbeing Indicator defined by the Wellbeing of Future Generations (Wales) Act 2015. The required OPD footprint is 2.4gha per person per year, with a clear trajectory to reduce this further to around 1.88 gha per person. Far more than creating low-impact homes, following this policy has positive social and ecological impacts. It includes building zero-carbon homes (embodied and operational), enhancing biodiversity and creating new habitats, producing around a third of food on site, dealing with own waste, and harvesting water. While it is relatively early days and challenging to achieve, it bravely exists, with most OPD households achieving the 2.4gha target early. Many homes offer tours and open days to share learning.

Carmarthenshire-based architect Mark Waghorn and his team design, prefabricate and assemble on site modular homes which follow the OPD guideline requirements. Sitting lightly on the land, they avoid the use of embodied-carbon-heavy traditional brick, steel and concrete. Instead, each building is framed and clad in carbon-sequestering, local, sustainably managed Welsh timber and has a green roof with native plants. Homes are available in one- or two-bedroom sizes, and the portal frame structure is designed to be extendable at a later date with minimal disruption.

The energy-efficient design has a reduced energy demand by being airtight and extra-insulated with wood-fibre insulation, having triple-glazed windows and doors, and using LED lighting – and it can be powered by solar photovoltaic panels or other micro-generation

10.1 House entrance, green roof and smallholding.

‘One Planet Development is a brave planning policy unique to Wales that is based on an honest appraisal of the combined climate breakdown and ecological crises facing us, and allows inspiring, positive responses that create a space for hope. Wales can act as an inspiration to others around the world. It is a beautiful land, rich in natural resources, with so many citizens who are making great efforts to facilitate positive change - to turn words into action. Understanding the importance of OPD requires the courage to face the reality of the situation, as only then can we appreciate the level of change needed in the way society operates.’

Mark Waghorn, Director, MWD Architects.[8]

options, including wind and micro hydro. The south-facing positioning provides solar gain in the winter. Prevailing winds from the southwest flow through the opened south/southwest-facing glazing and north/northeast-facing clerestory windows, allowing good cross ventilation on normal summer days. On very hot days, everything can be closed to exclude hot external air – the solar shading is critical to keep out solar gain so mechanical cooling isn't required. Airtightness is important so that heat isn't lost unnecessarily on windy, cold days, and the shading above south-facing windows limits the heat gain in the summer. From November to February, there's a biomass stove with a back boiler, which is primarily needed for hot water, with background space heating a few times a week.

To minimise each home's water footprint, rainwater harvesting is maximised and used for most water needs, alongside using natural water sources and human made sources such as a well or direct mains water. The bathroom and kitchen are fitted with water-saving devices. Gently used greywater from basin, shower, bath, sink and washing machine is used for irrigation.

Prefabrication off-site in their factory means optimal speed of production and material efficiency, as well as increased safety for workers. It also means, if needed, the home can be reused and relocated in the future. Internal walls could be hempcrete plaster made from hemp and lime, but these are generally avoided in favour of locally sourced, sustainably managed tongue-and-groove timber cladding boards, which travel easily and extend the life and ability to move the house at a later date. The foundations are screw piles, which can be easily unscrewed, and the land is then returned to a natural state.

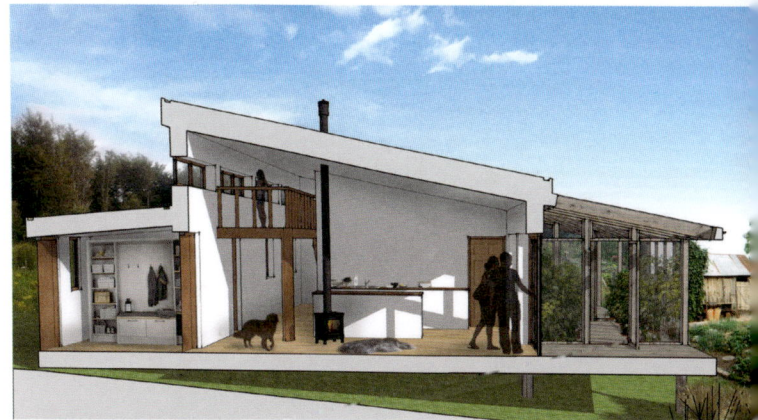

10.2 Cross section through Mark Waghorn's OPD modular home design.

10.3 South-facing elevation, with veranda and shading above.

FACTS

Founded: 2010

Founder: Mark Waghorn

Visit: www.mwd.wales

The interior design industry's impact on nature

The interior design industry has a multitude of impacts upon nature, entwined with climate change. Before we even look at processing, manufacturing and transportation, the growing, farming and extraction of materials used by our industry directly impacts biodiversity ecosystems, stripping land, waterways and oceans – and leading to the loss of natural habitats. Some examples are below.

Mining and quarrying

The scarred landscape in the Lumen Prize-winning rendered image by artist Dillon Marsh illustrates the former Jubilee copper mine in South Africa – the 6,500 tonnes of copper extracted over the quarry's lifetime is represented as a sphere. It's a stark reminder of the impact on land and biodiversity of resource extraction, along with the amount of waste the extraction of copper generates.

As architect Duncan Baker-Brown says in his TEDx talk, when highlighting the miserable working conditions of some open-cast copper mines, 'You try building without copper.'[9] Well, try specifying interior finishes without using marble, granite, limestone, sandstone, clay, slate and many other mined and quarried metals. Our industry undeniably has an impact.

Characteristically, these mineral extraction sites are in the middle of countryside. To address this erosion of nature, the Royal Society for the Protection of Birds (RSPB) programme Nature After Minerals (NAM) has been working with the quarrying industry in the UK for nearly two decades to rewild former quarry sites to be habitat havens for a large variety of species and provide nature for people to visit. These collaborations influence and strategise quarry restoration plans, habitat connectivity and creation of habitat for declining wildlife species. The RSPB has been collaborating with CEMEX to rewild 50 quarries in the UK and improve biodiversity conservation across CEMEX's 400 quarrying sites worldwide. Incidentally, the strapline used by the RSPB of 'giving nature a home' was replaced with a poignant new alarm call of Nature is in crisis. Together, we can save it' in July 2022, recognising the urgency to restore nature habitats.

Soil health

Something I had not fully appreciated until writing this book was the critical importance of soil health. Caring for and protecting this precious resource acts to address both climate change and biodiversity loss. If we continue to neglect our depleted soil health, we know we have shockingly limited harvests left, with some claiming it could be as few as 60 years.[10]

Moving to organically farmed fabric fibres and away from humanmade fertilisers and pesticides both improves soil health and stores enough carbon in the soil to keep the world within 1.5°C of global boiling.[11] In addition, most humanmade pesticides and fertilisers are fossil-fuel derived chemicals whose production releases CO_2e, which is then trapped in our atmosphere, causing global boiling. Overuse of these chemicals is described as causing catastrophic harm, not only to soil, but also to wildlife, rivers, plants and our food.[12] Below-ground biodiversity is part of the vital ecosystem which supports above-ground biodiversity. Soil is one of the largest reservoirs of biodiversity on Earth.[13]

Tree cover

Tree cover loss, through deforestation, illegal logging and fires, is also an enormous threat to biodiversity, to nature's own carbon-capturing ability, and contributes to global boiling.

Deforestation, the intentional clearance or reduction of woodland and forests to convert to other land uses, is responsible for about 15% of global greenhouse gas emissions.[14] European Union law requires manufacturers working in deforestation hotspots to certify that their goods have not harmed forests after a cut-off date of 31 December 2020. The list includes wood, charcoal, rubber, soya, beef, palm oil, cocoa, coffee and derived products including leather, furniture and chocolate.

Illegal logging, the harvesting of timber in violation of the law and regulations of a country, is the third most profitable transnational crime behind counterfeiting and drug trafficking.[15] Illegal logging is reported to account for 15 to 30% of the global timber trade and provides unfair competition through cheap, illegal wood supply.[16]

As we face huge deforestation and illegal logging, knowing that the sources of new timber and paper products are sustainably managed with a chain of custody is vital to ensuring habitats are protected and carbon is captured. Among the international certifications available to use are Forestry Stewardship Council (FSC®) and Programme for the Endorsement of Forest Certification (PEFC).

10.4 Dillon Marsh's prize-winning rendered image of the former Jubilee copper mine in South Africa.

HempWood ®

Murray, Kentucky, USA

Wonder fibre hemp is another form of nature's carbon capture. Fast-growing hemp plants take only five months to mature to the same level of carbon-capturing ability as a young forest. The crop sequesters twice as much carbon as trees, permanently into its fibres, with 1ha absorbing 9 to 16 tonnes of CO_2e.[17] It's a hardy plant that doesn't require pesticides to grow, requires minimal water, is a bio-accumulator cleaning up toxic chemicals and regenerates soil fertility.

We can wear it, eat it, drink it and use it in our cosmetics and toiletries. Henry Ford even developed a car built from a super-tough bioplastic made from hemp, flax, wheat and spruce pulp and fuelled by hemp. Rembrandt painted on hemp canvas. The first fabrics made from this plant fibre were by the ancient Chinese. The first Levi jeans were made from hemp fibre cloth. Hemp was central to maritime history as it was used for early rope and sailcloth.

We can live in it. Hemp has many uses within the built environment. We can construct, insulate, finish and furnish buildings with it. And yet versatile hemp has been so misunderstood and confused with its cousin marijuana, which has severely impeded its use.

Anita Roddick said of hemp, 'It didn't make rational sense to me that the extraordinary benefits this plant can supply were being so vilified. It is only ignorance that confuses hemp with marijuana.'[18]

The use of hemp in the US has boomed since the 2018 amendment to the Farm Bill legalising the agricultural growth of the crop. Innovator Greg Wilson, founder of the company Fibonacci, had been experimenting for many years with fibres. He had the HempWood® patent approved after developing and refining the process to reverse-engineer hemp as a timber substitute composite and combining it with a soya-based glue he'd developed. Using locally farmed hemp, the product has no added formaldehyde and is chemical free, using

10.5 HempWood® Organic Flooring in Natural finish.

10.6 HempWood® Organic Flooring in Marble finish.

The multi-award-winning affordable housing research project PA Hemp Home, designed by Parsons Healthy Materials Lab (HML), is a collaboration between non-profit DON Enterprise and the Penn State University Housing Research Center. The objective for the project was to renovate a century-old family home, affordably, using healthy building materials. The Parsons team was looking for a benign, non-toxic and regenerative materials to use. Engineered timber flooring sparingly uses high-grade timber more efficiently, and combined with the cross lamination of layers, makes it a stable solution. However, the toxic petrochemical glues generally used to bind the layers have been problematic to human and ecological health, in use and at end of life. The team from Parsons HML found HempWood®, made just 15 minutes away from the project, and used it throughout the home. It also used hempcrete (hemp lime) spray-applied insulation, with a richer hemp–lime mix for the interior finish, painted in lime wash. Porcelain tiles were used for tiled areas. The home's building ecosystem is being monitored and tested for indoor air quality, energy and performance.

a soya-based adhesive. The plywood backing is FSC® certified, and formaldehyde and VOC free. The product can be used in place of timber, with its initial application being for flooring. It takes just 150 days to produce, from seed germination to flooring. With a 2,200 Janka hardness rating, it is harder and more durable than hardwood, and resistant to wear, scratches and dents.

HempWood® has been certified by the United States Department of Agriculture (USDA) and carries their Bio Preferred product label.It comes in two grades of character, four colours, finished or unfinished. The manufacturing process has a low waste percentage of 15% and this waste is used as a biofuel for the factory; experiments to use the waste in a new external product are underway. The dependence on fossil fuels has been lessened by strategically locating the factory next to the hemp-growing region and by a river for hydro power.

FACTS

Founded: 2018

Founder: Greg Wilson

Awards: Kentucky Agri Tech Business of the Year 2022

Certifications: USDA Bio-Preferred, LCA, EPD and ASTM 1037

Visit: Showroom: 301 Rockwood Road, Murray, KY 42071, USA, www.hempwood.com

10.7 The Plus sits on the very edge of Vestre's factory site, taking up only 5%, preserving the forest in the remainder of the site.

10.8 The spiral ramp in the centre courtyard of the building; the celebrated tree can be viewed from each wing of the building.

10.9 Architect Viktoria Millentrup on the roof of The Plus.

The Plus

Magnor, Norway

As the chapter is about the climate and biodiversity crisis, I should start by writing about how The Plus sits on a modest footprint, removing the minimal amount of pine trees. It nestles within the forest that tightly surrounds it, and the forest floor has been transferred onto the roof and further enriched with native flora and fauna. Or I should write about how the timber building uses timber from pine trees felled to create the site, is a store for 1,400 tonnes of carbon and is built to Passive House standards. Or how the project brief for this building was to make the most suitable furniture factory in the world. I will tell you all about these things, but what I really want to tell you first is how joyful, accessible and fun The Plus is. It's so easy to forget this is a factory at all.

Much thought has been given to making the experience of Vestre's furniture factory enjoyable for both employees and visitors. How many factories have the nation's highest slide, or a Forest Camp complete with children's playground, including oversized versions of Vestre's urban furniture, and also art and sculpture trails with poems by national favourite Hans Bjørl on each object? Norway's ancient *Allemannsretten* right to roam was enshrined in law in 1957. 'Everyman's right' ensures access to nature for all, to uncultivated land. This means hikers will be passing and people could be camping in the forest, so externally accessed bathroom facilities are provided, and campers are welcomed in for a morning coffee. The factory is glazed, with a perimeter path for visitors to walk around the building to watch the factory's processes in action. Visitors access the roof by steps or a ramp for views across the forest and inside the building. From the roof, a spiralled ramp leads to the courtyard, where there's a Norwegian maple *Acer platanoides* tree in the middle, as an axis mundi, of connection to earth and global connectivity. We haven't even got inside the building yet.

Vestre's furniture is made to last, with long guarantees. It is easy to repair with permanently available spare parts, and products can be returned for refurbishment in Vestre's service loop. Vestre products are each CO_2e calculated for ease of evaluation when specifying. All come with Environmental Product Declarations (EPDs) for transparency, and many have the Nordic Swan Ecolabel which is the official ecolabel for products from Nordic countries. The materials used in Vestre's furniture are carefully sourced. The company uses sustainably managed Scandinavian pine, and Hydro CIRCAL, a 75%-minimum-recycled post-consumer scrap aluminium which has a CO_2e footprint of below 2.3kgCO_2e per 1kg, compared to primary aluminium which can be many times higher, depending where in the world it is made. Vestre is the first furniture manufacturer in the world to use Swedish SSAB fossil-free steel in its products.

The company has always been family owned and was founded after World War II, producing urban furniture for global customers. Production had outgrown the existing factory in Torsby, just across the border in Sweden. The Plus at Magnor would become home to Vestre's woodwork, powder coating and assembly factory, with Torsby used for making steel and aluminium components, with biodiesel trucks running between the two sites. Architect Viktoria Millentrup was asked to lead the project for Bjarke Ingels Group (BIG). She was excited at the prospect of creating a factory in the forest, a certified sustainability project for BIG, and her first building to be constructed. She knew Vestre's strong values and high expectations for the sustainability, quality and design of its furniture products and was excited to deliver a building design that matched these ethics as well.

The first step was the site. The forest was originally going to be felled for a huge industrial development. To Vestre and the BIG team, using the smallest site footprint was important. They chose to locate the building on the edge of the site, leaving the remaining 95% of the forest to grow wild, providing a home for nature. Working closely with the local council and Vestre's ecology consultants, refuges for wildlife have been added. The design was to be conscious of this ecosystem that the building fits within, along with not wanting dependency on fossil fuels or causing pollution to the biodiversity through air, water and soil. Water use has been considered throughout, including storm water, water used in the building's operation and water used in production by the factory's painting process, of which 90% is recycled in a closed loop, greatly reducing consumption.

The team has created an interior experience that is exciting for employees and visitors. From the centre courtyard extend four main production hall wings. The layout provides an efficient shape for the flow of the production process. Each wing is colour coded and each machine has a colour, using 24 of Vestre RAL colours used on the products. These colours playfully run along the floors to show the workflow, both practical to use and fun for the visitors to observe. Employees have a bright, airy and colourful environment, with views of the forest.

Oslo-based design duo Anderssen & Voll, who have designed some of the furniture within Vestre's product range, worked on the interior furnishing fit-out. Knowing their client's ethos well already, they designed and specified low-impact and locally made pieces for the reception, meeting rooms, lunch area and office space. They did this using their own furniture, as well as other Scandinavian manufacturers, design classics from Vitra, and preloved refurbished furniture from Glomma Industrier. Floors on the first floor are finished in pine to match the construction timber seen in the interior.

Taking less than 18 months to construct, The Plus has been certified BREEAM 'Outstanding' and also meets Vestre's Paris Agreement goal of cutting greenhouse gas emissions by 40% by 2030 compared to similar buildings. The building itself emits 55% less GHG emissions through its energy efficiency and the materials used: low-carbon concrete, recycled reinforcing steel and timber. The same recycled aluminium used in the furniture was used in for the glazing profiles, locally supplied by Vestre's neighbour. The factory is powered by 888 photovoltaic solar panels, supplemented with renewable grid energy until a ground-based solar plant is added later. The building is heated and cooled using heat pumps and geothermal wells. Machinery running in the factory is fossil-fuel free and emission free.

10.10 Colour coding on the factory floors showing the workflow through the factory.

10.11 The production wing, with a long staircase leading to the first floor.

10.12 The slide from the factory roof. At 15m, it is Norway's highest, and a reminder of Vestre's early beginnings, when it made playground equipment as well as outdoor furtniture.

10.13 Children joyfully running up the stairs to the slide, enjoying the tourist attraction which is the Vestre factory building

As well as being a world-leading building that demonstrates the company's integrity and authenticity, much to the delight of the founder's grandson, Jan Christian, who initiated this huge project, has achieved his goal for it to be a tourist attraction, featuring on TripAdvisor. It's so easy to forget this is actually a factory.

FACTS

Client: Vestre Group

Architect, interior design and lighting design: BIG Bjarke Ingels Group ApS

Interior design (loose inventory): Anderssen & Voll

Ecology consultants: Asplan Viak

Completion: 2022

Gross internal floor area: 7,000m²

Visit: The Plus, Gaustadvegen 140, 2240 Magnor, Norway

explore

Architects Declare, Practice Guide: www.architectsdeclare.com

The Construction Material Pyramid – quick-reference chart demonstrating CO2 values for building materials, www.materialepyramiden.dk

Interior Design Declares – a network of interior design practices, suppliers of goods and services, www.interiordesigndeclares.com

International Monetary Fund, 'One-on-one with Christine Lagarde, featuring Sir David Attenborough: Balancing Nature and the Global Economy', 11 April 2019, https://meetings.imf.org/en/2019/Spring/Schedule/2019/04/11/imf-seminar-one-on-one-lagarde

International Union for Conservation of Nature (IUCN), Red List of Threatened Species, www.iucnredlist.org

Parson's Healthy Materials Lab, Trace Material podcast, series 1, 'Hemp'.

Timber:

Forest Stewardship Council, www.fsc.org

Programme for the Endorsement of Forest Certification, www.pefc.org

Preferred By Nature – sources of legal timber and the risk score for each country, www.preferredbynature.org/sourcinghub/timber

Wellbeing of Future Generations (Wales) Act 2015, www.futuregenerations.wales

11

Ethical Business

> ❝ Governance, transparency and accountability is the cornerstone of ethical practice and ethical business.
>
> You cannot deliver social impact and environmental innovation without a process that brings together all stakeholders and feedback systems to hold an organisation accountable. With it comes an openness to learn, to create and collaborate with supplier partners, customers, employees and other stakeholders.
> It requires creativity and discipline.❞

Safia Minney, social entrepreneur and author[1]

Long-standing ethical businesses which combine ecology and economy are now shining brightly as leaders. They have forged the way against the tide of profit-first businesses and survived and thrived, showing that business can make profit while also being regenerative to people, planet and animals. This model for the new paradigm has proved businesses can be successful while being interconnected with nature, and can work collaboratively at scale and at pace on solutions to lessen impact.

While running People Tree's biannual Social Reviews, Safia Minney, Founder and CEO, sat an Earth cushion globe at the table to represent bringing Mother Earth into the review process and action plan formation, as a key stakeholder. 'It's easy to forget when her voice can't be heard over human voices, but she is the giver of all life and I hoped with her being there we would be reminded to make decisions for the business framed by ecology and our limited natural resources,'[2] Minney said.

Ethics are attractive to consumers who increasingly recognise movements like Certified B Corporations™ which encourage businesses to operate responsibly – considering community and environment in everything they do.

Here, businesses join a community to grow, share learnings, support each other and improve together. Administered and verified by B Labs in more than 70 countries, B Corp™ recertification is required every three years, each time exceeding the previous B Impact score. The freely accessible Impact Assessment is where companies can start to submit information and see where to improve before going ahead with the application process.

I'm heartened by the surge in businesses who voluntarily want to be ethical and actively share knowledge with others to do the same. I am purposely not calling this chapter ESG (Environmental, Social and Governance) or CSR (Corporate Social Responsibility) as both feel they come from a dutiful place as they are gradually required by company law for large business, rather than being based on a motivated desire to be ethical and values driven. Third-party certifications, standards and accreditations are available to support ethical business, such as ISO 14001, the international standard for an environmental management system.

There are so many ways to improve ethics in business without the complexities of any certification. Looking into finances, who a business banks with, insures with and where pensions are invested have a huge impact on carbon emissions and social impact. Interior designers have a big influence on supply chains and we should use it by being inquisitive, pushing for transparency and avoidance of fossil fuels, in order to reduce impact, collectively if needed.

The Sustainable Development Goals (SDGs) Action Manager tool is a helpful free resource for any business to self-track their sustainable development. The SDGs were adopted by 193 countries of the United Nations general assembly in 2015 to action and achieve by 2030. These 17 SDGs provide goals and 169 smaller targets for business to commit to and measure against, by starting with the goals that are most relevant and using the SDGs Action Manager tool to monitor progress, set goals and communicate them.

11.1 Portable zigzag display shelving designed for the Goodee at the Whitney shop.

Goodee at the Whitney

New York City, USA

Multi-award-winning multidisciplinary studio Sangaré, based in Montreal, is led by industrial designer Nicholas Sangaré. As the company has developed it has moved from residential interiors to retail, with the team now working on hotel concepts. The studio researches and develops materials and processes to widen their specification range and experiment more deeply in concepts. Sangaré started an offshoot business named Isle to develop a range of product designs used in his spaces, such as handles, bathroom accessories, mailboxes, shelves, hooks and lighting, which are Canadian made and sold online.

Two initiatives have been of support to Sangaré's team. Index Design showcases design talent in the province of Quebec and encourages collaboration and knowledge sharing among the community. There is also Design Montréal, a local government strategy for development of design and architecture to enhance the quality of living in the city, complete with a toolkit of best practices to follow.

Pursuing the B Corp™ certification was a very natural step for Sangaré as the team were doing much of it already, such as using local suppliers and materials regularly. Sangaré has found sustainability is not easy to associate with luxury interiors, although sustainability results from the use of high-end materials. B Corp™ certification attracts and communicates with likeminded clients who appreciate ethical business and therefore there is no need to educate every client. Sangaré is currently preparing for the third-year B Corp™ recertification and is setting new goals for further improvement, sharing learnings within the design community.

Twin brothers, Byron and Dexter Peart, founded Goodee, a much-loved, growing Canadian online platform selling consciously sourced craft, with a particular emphasis on protecting endangered crafts and the livelihoods that depend on them.

As well as being a Certified B Corporation™, Goodee has chosen SDGs to align to, supporting its values of 'good design, good people and good purpose' around nurturing people (5 Gender Equality, 10 Reduced Inequalities), cultural heritage (4 Quality Education, 8 Decent Work and Economic Growth) and planet (12 Responsible Consumption and Production, 13 Climate Action).

11.2 Pine storage units, shelving with yellow dividers and pendant lighting from Goodee's retail offering.

11.3 Table top in Durat, a repairable, long-lasting terrazzo solid surfacing made from plastic waste collected in Finland and Sweden, and manufactured using 100% renewable energy.

The brothers were invited by the Whitney Museum to transition from e-commerce to a retail space selling 'The Whitney edit', with a condensed, curated collection of their home decor to run alongside the museum's *Making Knowing: Craft in Art, 1950–2019* exhibition. It was important they chose the right designers to help them achieve and convey their values. Goodee, which is also Montréal-based, approached the team at Sangaré to be the partners for the project. They were given a tight timeline of a month to design, manufacture and install the concept, which needed to convey the character and values of the brand while having a different identity to the museum's permanent shop.

Led by Nicholas Sangaré, the team devised a distinctive design from a simple palette of four easily disassembled component materials.

Their portable kiosk design is based around mobile display tables which double as a workshop area, with metal-framed zigzag folding shelving units for further retail display and to demark the area. They used knotty FSC®-certifed pine shelves as textured background for the handmade pieces displayed on them, brand yellow acrylic dividers and recycled plastic Durat for the table tops. Decorative pendant lights for the retail area are taken from Goodee's range, made by Eperara-Siapidara artisans originating from west Colombia, created from colourful natural-pig-ment-dyed palm strips woven around an upcycled PET bottle.

Sangaré's pop-up store for Goodee at the Whitney is much loved by patrons and is still there, even though the exhibition finished in early 2022. The design has been replicated for an in-store kiosk roll-out for retailer Nordstrom and the original is on display in the Goodee head-quarters, ready to be reused as a pop-up again, and again.

FACTS

Client: Goodee

Interior design: Sangaré

Completion: 2019

Gross internal floor area: 20m²

Visit: The Whitney Museum of American Art, 99 Gansevoort Street. New York, NY 10014, USA

skinflint

Penryn, Cornwall, UK

Convincing a client that the original features of their home could be beautifully mixed together with utilitarian vintage light fittings was the point that skinflint started in 2009. The project for this client had initiated a search for suitable preloved fittings around the UK, and resulted in an impressive aesthetic loved by the client, as well as storytelling of antiqueness and provenance that comes with the process. Through this project, skinflint's founders realised they had a created a passion project with a purpose. They began to salvage light fittings from factories, shipbreakers' yards, hospitals, theatres, warehouses and churches, saving them from landfill: in essence, starting a business in rescuing, repairing and restoring.

The founders, Chris and Sophie Miller, have very different interiors-related backgrounds. Setting up their riverside studio in Penryn, in Cornwall, meant there was a ready-made community network of local small workshops serving the yacht industry, with the very services they needed to bring their finds back to life: repairing, sympathetic restoration and rewiring. More recently, ethical start-up companies have joined them in the area.

The company is aware of its impact on the planet and its stakeholders, and sees restoring vintage lights as an act of care, describing itself as 'thinkers, makers, doers and shakers, working together to make business a force for good'.

The company's chosen SDGs to align with their ethics are '8 Decent Work and Economic Growth', '10 Reduced Inequalities', '12 Responsible Consumption and Production' and '13 Climate Action'.

All parts of the business's impact are scrutinised. It has been B Corp™ certified since December 2021 and is working on further improvements for recertification. It is working to be carbon neutral in 2025, achieved through continuingly goal setting, measuring and reduction, offsetting what is left through a Gold Standard scheme. Their sourcing trips, whether nationally or internationally, are by train or boat. Employees are given two extra days' leave for travelling on holiday in a sustainable way. People are valued over profit. Skinflint is a Real Living Wage employer, ensuring its team earns a wage that's enough to live on. It wants its team to enjoy being at work, so regularly take time out for team away days, including fishing trips, go-karting, long lunches and seaweed foraging — ideas driven by and voted upon by the team. Employees are also encouraged to take volunteering days, spending time contributing to projects that they're passionate about.

Skinflint specialises in rescuing and reviving electric light fittings made between 1920 and 1970. During the sympathetic restoration that keeps the high-quality originals from landfill, lamp holders are converted to take LED lamps. These renovated lights continue to be perfect examples of the circular economy in practice as they have a lifetime guarantee, which includes repairs, along with an award-winning 'Full Circle' buyback scheme. This gives customers a 50% credit for future purchases and ensures the fittings stay in the Use Cycle loop for their next chapter after being repaired, restored and recertified. Their restored vintage lights are in shops, hotels, offices and private residences, both internationally and in the UK, from fellow Certified B Corporations™ like Patagonia and Aesop, to pioneering breweries like Verdant Brewing Company.

'There is no magic wand to Net Zero, but we are certainly taking small steps along that long and twisty road.'

James Heffron, Head Brewer and Cofounder, Verdant Brewing Company[3]

Independent Cornish craft beer brewer Verdant is well loved and had been growing in popularity so needed to expand its brewery and offices. It found a rundown warehouse on an industrial estate in Penryn where it could have a taproom as well. The brewery's founders chose to work with James Collins, whose local architectural and interior design practice Zelah Studio shares the company's values for reducing impact and a strong desire to support the Cornish economy by using as many local suppliers and tradespeople as possible.

11.5 Verdant Brewing Taproom, Penryn, Cornwall.

11.6 The ground-floor seating area of the Verdant Brewing Taproom, with a bar at the rear.

The revival and reuse of the building included extra insulation in occupied areas, a 65kW solar insulation providing all the power, along with electric car charging for company and staff vehicles, and a heat recovery system, installed to minimise the need for heating. In terms of materiality, the scheme minimised material palette and use, relying on existing elements of the industrial structure. Sustainably sourced ply formed the basis for most of the internal structures and furniture. A large planter in the atrium space was filled with air-cleansing plants, whose organic shapes soften the hard lines of the design. Views through to the working brewery were important. The space needed to be multifunctional to serve the local community as well as hosting DJ nights, cinema screenings, gigs, comedy, music and restaurant pop-ups.

Collins' film set design experience, coupled with the careful placement of the reconditioned vintage light fittings in the lighting design, provide a theatrical effect. The design is versatile to suit the multiple uses of the space. The intelligent lighting system throughout means the office lights change colour with the time of day to optimise the working environment, creating a natural, 'unlit' feeling, while the bar settings create an ambient light. All this is controlled with iPads from anywhere in the building. The lifetime guarantee of the reconditioned lights and the buyback scheme reassured the clients of the extended life cycle of the product. The project went on to be a regional winner of the British Institute of Interior Design Awards.

FACTS

skinflint

Founded: 2009

Founders: Chris Miller, Sophie Miller
Certifications: Certified B Corporation

Visit: Showroom (appointment only), The Warehouse, Commercial Road, Penryn, Cornwall, TR10 8AE
www.skinflintdesign.com

Client: Verdant Brewing Company

Interior design: Zelah Studio

Lighting designer: skinflint

Completion: 2022

Gross internal floor area: 215m², plus 140m² of offices

Visit: Verdant Brewing Taproom, 30 Parkengue, Kernick Industrial Estate, Penryn TR10 9EP, UK, www.verdantbrewing.co

11.7 skinflint's 1950s Eastern Bloc machinist light.
11.8 The bar, with skinflint vintage Czech pendants.

11.9 The Body Shop's Changemakers' Workshop concept.

The Body Shop, Changemakers' Workshop global store design

multiple locations

> ❜ I don't give a toss about being a bigger company, I care about becoming a better company, a more values-driven company.'

Anita Roddick, Business As Unusual[4]

The Body Shop was founded in 1976 by Anita Roddick in Brighton, UK. From this small shop with a purpose, Roddick started something revolutionary, where a global business with a triple bottom line (of people, planet and profit) could be a force for good. The Body Shop solidly continues to be a vehicle for campaigning and change-making, a purpose which strongly drives the company over four decades later. Pioneering in the retail sector, Roddick championed Community Fair Trade, animal rights and was a forerunner of the refill revolution: challenging the beauty industry to be inclusive and empowering.

Working for an ethical business can attract, motivate and retain staff. I am a prime example of this – I grew up with The Body Shop as it started in my hometown. It was an exciting place to shop and through visiting during my teens, I learnt about important global issues as The Body Shop partnered with Greenpeace, Friends of the Earth, Amnesty International and then initiated its own ground-breaking Against Animal Testing campaign, which led the way to a European Union-wide ban on animal testing in 2013. Three generations of my family shopped there. By the time I had graduated in design and after an unsuccessful start as a junior designer during a recession, I wrote to Anita Roddick for help. She gave me work experience at The Body Shop's highly creative and inspiring design office in London and then I went on to have a 10-year career with the company, working on projects globally. I was a Values Champion,

where team members were from across the business rather than in a separate department. Upholding the company's ethics was not a box-ticking exercise. There were no certifications and accreditations to be a part of at that time. It was all self-motivated and inspiring to be a part of.

Many employees joined for the ethics and stayed because they were engaged in the business, and were valued. Now, an innovative Open Hiring model introduced in some markets in 2021 is removing barriers to employment while focusing on inclusivity and potential. The company has evidently always had a special way of operating in business, and it feels very natural that this ethos carried into my own interior design business, which I set up upon leaving.

In her book *Body and Soul*, Roddick revealed:

> *I am still looking for the modern-day equivalent of those Quakers who ran successful businesses, made money because they offered honest products and treated their people decently, worked hard, spent honestly, saved honestly, gave honest value for money, put back more than they took out and told no lies. This business creed, sadly, seems long forgotten.[5]*

The key legal part of the B Corp™ process is to change the Articles of Association, the public expression of a business, to state that through its business and operations, the company was to have a material positive impact on society and the environment.[6] Some 25 years before B Corp™ had even begun, Roddick and her husband Gordon changed the Articles of Association for The Body Shop by dedicating the legal purpose of their business to pursue social and environmental change and human rights advocacy.[7] At time of writing, The Body Shop has gone on to be the world's largest Certified B Corporation™ as part of its parent company Natura &Co.

The retail environments have always played a crucial role in communicating the company's purpose. As with the products the company makes and sells, the specifications used in the store designs also convey the business's ethics. To the present day, the

11.10 The store interior, with exposed ceiling and existing lighting, along with a product demonstration area and display trestle tables.

business continues to use regenerative products such as hemp and organic cotton. It avoids any polyvinyl chloride (PVC), only sustainable FSC®-certified timber is used, and formaldehyde, glues and paints containing animal derivatives are all avoided – as well, of course, as products tested on animals. Some of the merchandising equipment was made by Community Fair Trade suppliers who the company has maintained especially long-standing relationships with. Experimental materials are used, especially reused and repurposed ones, supporting small, innovative makers such as One Foot Taller, Made of Waste and Smile Plastics in their very early days. Everything specified is checked against the self-set list of materials, production globally is vetted and visited to ensure factories are safe places to work and do not cause harm to communities or ecology, and

workers are treated fairly and equitably. In the time I was there, the retail design team took the simple, early 'green box' design to a UK's Retail Week award-winning concept.

This industry-leading work goes on. In the years since, the subsequent retail design concepts have continued to win awards, be scrutinised, pushed further and improved. The global retail design team impressively pushes the ethics at scale (across both company and franchise markets), working with and challenging their global shopfitting manufacturers and installation stakeholders.

The company's new store concept, 'Changemakers' Workshop', is the most sustainable and values-aligned store concept for the company to date and is in the process of being rolled out globally. These stores are community spaces, where the company's purpose is brought to life, by bringing people together to campaign for positive change and discover the human story of the ethically sourced products.

The concept is a great example of dematerialisation, as in doing more with less and utilising what is already present in the original architecture of the host retail shell. Where possible, floors and walls are unchanged, and ceilings are left exposed and therefore easily accessible for maintenance. Through responsible sourcing, embodied carbon is reviewed and improved.

Where new materials are introduced, the material palette uses responsible, reclaimed or recycled materials that cause no harm to people, animals or the planet. Some 90% of the wood, metal, plastic and glass used in this store design is more sustainable than previous store designs. All new timber continues to be FSC®-certified, with factories also FSC®-accredited for the full chain of custody transparency. Multipurpose trestle tables are made from reclaimed timber and designed in conjunction with sheet cutting yields to minimise wastage. The team are actively sourcing new materials, such as 'Ekoply', a 100%-recycled plastic-sheet alternative which is used for surfaces.

The make-up stands previously had product-specific merchandising units made from injection-moulded virgin acrylic plastic; they are now redesigned to be simpler, modular, generic holders made from easily disassembled FSC® timber and steel. This future-proofed redesign means that for every 100 Workshop make-up stands, 9.5 tonnes of virgin acrylic plastic is saved.

While the operational carbon emitted through the energy use of the store's shell is often part of the lease, so not always easy to influence, other areas were possible to improve. General lighting is as the lease provides. Where possible, reused lighting and recycled aluminium LED spotlights are added to key areas as needed.

11.11 The Changemaking Act area, where customers can support campaigns for positive change; seen alongside the refill station, which is part of a global roll-out to encourage refilling of reusable aluminium packaging.

11.12 The plastic-free Workshop make-up stand.

Every fixture has been designed to include the whole life cycle. In addition to using materials that cause no harm to people, animals or the planet, every fixture can be recycled or repurposed. No materials are bonded together; everything is mechanically fixed for easy disassembly. Each fixture has a QR code product passport label which accesses information on the design and maintenance, which enables informed decisions about end-of-life disposal.

Supplier selection at The Body Shop is carefully managed before work begins. All first-tier manufacturers are Supplier Ethical Data Exchange (SEDEX) registered to maintain data on ethical and responsible practices for transparency in the supply chain. Manufacturers' working conditions require a SEDEX Members Ethical Trade Audit (SMETA). The relationship with manufacturers is therefore critical to the successful delivery of store fit-outs on a global scale.

 As part of the continuous improvement commitment, shop fit is assessed, measured and scored. Materials are scored using Building Research Establishment (BRE) 'Ecopoints'. Fixtures are scored using the Sustain® tool score for measuring carbon, water or any other relevant metric, enabling the retailer to actively measure carbon savings alongside cost when evaluating any value engineering, so delivering to their full triple-bottom-line intent. In the 2020 review, 68% of the fixtures in the store concept scored an A or A+ Ecopoints rating.

The work of five decades at The Body Shop continues to build pace. As the roll-out continues, the store concept is constantly being pushed to find more ways to lessen its impact by working collaboratively with all stakeholders – manufacturers and global teams. The business as a whole is encouraged by the three-yearly B Corp™ recertification and a firm 2030 net zero 'Commitment for Life' which includes the Scope 3 indirect emissions[8] throughout the entire supply chain, complete with a clear roadmap to achieve it. The positive ripples from this pioneering and influential ethical business radiate far further than the company itself.

11.13 The cash-and-wrap area, one of the areas in store where the work of local artists, ceramists and printmakers within the community is displayed.

FACTS

Founded: 1976

Founders: Anita and Gordon Roddick

Certifications: Certified B Corporation, 'Vegan Certified' The Vegan Society trademark

Visit: www.thebodyshop.com

explore

UN Sustainable Development Goals (SDGs) Action Manager tool, www.bcorporation.net/en-us/programs-and-tools/sdg-action-manager

Isle, www.isle-store.ca

LEARNINGS

1 **INFLUENCE.** Clients engage us for our expertise and knowledge. Push their boundaries. Use this book to show them that sustainable interiors can also look great. Working with the supply chain, upstream and downstream from you, will really stimulate change. Be open to conversation. Don't underestimate your influence and buying power. If we act collectively our supply chains will be more quickly responsive. Questions cause ripples of demand and those suppliers with good business-sense will respond to that demand.

2 **COLLABORATE.** With all the approaches I saw very similar examples of how they are incorporated into a project. Once defined, the project intent/approach needs to be clearly communicated and involve all stakeholders, ideally in the form of a charrette made up from the project's team and users of the space to work collaboratively together. It strikes me that when everyone is involved in a project at the very beginning, are all listened to and engaged, projects are hugely more successful. Encourage charrettes where all stakeholders have input from outset – including the vital building managers and cleaners who ensure the spaces handed over and continue to operate and be maintained as intended.

3 **SUPER MATERIALS.** Hemp and bamboo, both fast growing and regenerative to soil ecosystems, circular, organically grown, carbon sequestering, strong, durable., low water usage. I could easily have put hemp into every chapter. Bamboo when used with timber is a strong and regenerative alternative to traditional, carbon-heavy building materials.

4 **BE INQUISITIVE.** Toxic chemicals appear to be increasing in use and are evidently a rising problem to human and planetary health, plus toxic chemicals require animal testing. Benign and inert materials don't cause harm or need testing and they regenerate safely. An easy question to ask of suppliers is 'Is this Red List Free?' Question 'natural'. In the case of animal products, they are most often chemically treated to stop deterioration, and therefore are not regenerative. Pushing the boundaries causes more ripples of positive change than you realise as we move out of our familiar processes to try new ones.

5 **TRANSPARENCY.** Both product ingredients and manufacturing supply chain transparency is vital. Demand transparency from suppliers. They often don't know themselves. Make better choices by working with those who are transparent and reward them. We really do need harmonised, standardised common data in order to properly compare and evaluate.

6 **WHOLE LIFE CYCLE.** Waste is a result of poor design. Urge manufacturers to design products and materials with the whole life cycle. . Think of the full life cycle of a specification when selecting. Use third party certifications to navigate the choices, but don't only use certified products as smaller manufacturers can't always afford these certification processes.

7 **TECHNOLOGY.** Blockchain technology in our industry's supply chain must be the solution to raise standards and pay fairly. Artificial Intelligence (AI) will play an important role in efficiencies, optimising and monitoring resources and supply chains. Use of Materials Passports is already assisting extending the life of materials beyond their first use.

8 **SOIL.** It is vital that we must protect soil health. It plays the most essential part in human life on earth. Soil literally supports our survival, it is an essential part of our biodiversity ecosystem, it's our food source, and it's nature's solution to carbon sequestration and global boiling reduction. Support those organic farmers and supply chains whose processes protect and regenerate it.

9 **CONNECTION.** Connection to nature. Connect to community - buying locally. Connect with industry to encourage and influence change. Connect to your work and the life cycle of what is specified. Connect to those who are pushing boundaries and take a leap of faith, who are innovating, adapting and evolving in our industry by working with them. We need to encourage the experimenters. Doing the same things in the same way is not going to result in change. We all need to be open and willing to take some risks if change is going to happen.

10 **MAKE IT PERSONAL.** For me, aligning my personal values with how I work has been an extremely rewarding thing to do. Use this book to talk about an approach that fits your clients. Just start any way you can and don't wait to do it perfectly.

'NOTHING WILL HAPPEN AUTOMATICALLY. CHANGE DEPENDS ON WHAT YOU AND I DO EVERY DAY'

Gloria Steinem

MY FAVOURITE INSPIRATIONS

BOOKS

Geddes, L. *Chasing the Sun: The New Science of Sunlight and How it Shapes Our Bodies and Minds.* Wellcome Collection, London, 2019

Williams, F. *The Nature Fix: Why Nature Makes Us Happier, Healthier, And More Creative.* WW Norton & Co., New York City, 2017.

Berners-Lee, M. *How Bad Are Bananas? the Carbon Footprint of Everything.* Profile, London, 2010.

Minney, S. *Regenerative Fashion: A Nature-based Approach to Fibres, Livelihoods and Leadership.* Quercus Publishing, London, 2022.

Minney, S. *Slave to Fashion* New Internationalist Publications Ltd, London, 2017.

Potter, C. *Welcome to the Circular Economy: The next step in sustainable living.* Orion Publishing Co, London, 2021.

Fée, N. *How to Save The World For Free.* Orion Publishing Co, London, 2021.

Fée, N. *Do Good, Get Paid.* Orion Publishing Co, London, 2023.

Conway-Wood, S. *Buy Better Consume Less: Create Real Environmental Change.* Icon Books, London, 2022

Davidson, J. *#futuregen: Lessons from a Small Country.* Chelsea Green Publishing Co London, 2020.

DOCUMENTARIES

'Secret Life Of Landfill', television documentary, BBC, UK, broadcast 23 August 2018.

'Toxic Hot Seat', documentary, Zoetrope Aubry Productions, USA, 2013.

'Singapore: Biophilic City', film, Films For Action, USA, 2012.

'Pie Net Zero', short film, Spanner Films, UK, 2020

'Slay', feature documentary, *First Spark Media*, USA, 2022. www.slay.film

'The True Cost', feature documentary, *Untold Creative*, USA, 2016. www.truecostmovie.com

'Fashion Reimagined', feature documentary, *Together Films*, UK, 2022 www.fashionreimaginedfilm.com

OTHER

Earth Overshoot Day www.overshootday.org

Slavery Footprint www.slaveryfootprint.org

The House of Upcycling www.thehouseofupcycling.com

Endnotes

INTRODUCTION

1 Quote provided to the author for this publication.

2 BBC News, 'Pollution: Birds "ingesting hundreds of bits of plastic a day"', 22 May 2020, www.bbc.co.uk/news/science-environment-52762120 (accessed 18 November 2022).

3 Nina Renshaw, 'A healthy future for children and adolescents', *The Lancet*, 1 October 2022, www.thelancet.com/journals/lancet/article/PIIS0140-6736(22)01604-X/fulltext (accessed 18 November 2022). BBC News, 'Ella Adoo-Kissi-Debrah: Air pollution a factor in girl's death, inquest finds', 16 December 2020, www.bbc.co.uk/news/uk-england-london-55330945 (accessed 16 October 2023).

4 BBC News, 'UK heatwave: How do temperatures compare with 1976?', 19 July 2022, www.bbc.co.uk/news/62212604 (accessed 18 November 2022).

5 Damian Carrington, 'Microplastics found deep in lungs of living people for first time', *The Guardian*, 1 October 2021, www.theguardian.com/environment/2022/apr/06/microplastics-found-deep-in-lungs-of-living-people-for-first-time (accessed 18 November 2022).

6 Fidra, 'Flame-proof gannets: Tracing toxic chemicals through our wildlife', 8 June 2019, www.fidra.org.uk/news/flame-proof-gannets-tracing-toxic-chemicals-through-our-wildlife (accessed 18 November 2022).

7 World Health Association, 'Air pollution', www.who.int/health-topics/air-pollution#tab=tab_2 (accessed 18 November 2022).

8 NASA, 'NASA announces summer 2023 hottest on record', 14 September 2023, www.nasa.gov/news-release/nasa-announces-summer-2023-hottest-on-record/#:~:text=The%20summer%20of%202023%20was,(GISS)%20in%20New%20York (accessed 16 October 2023).

9 Maya Wei-Haas, 'Space junk is a huge problem – and it's only getting bigger', *National Geographic*, 25 April 2019, www.nationalgeographic.com/science/article/space-junk (accessed 18 November 2022).

10 Henry Cockburn, 'Rainwater everywhere on Earth contains cancer-causing "forever chemicals", study finds', *The Independent*, 2 August 2022, www.independent.co.uk/climate-change/news/rainwater-cause-cancer-forever-chemicals-pfas-b2137020.html (accessed 18 November 2022).

11 Natalie Fée, *How to Save the World for Free*, Laurence King Publishing, 2019, p 19.

12 Jack Wilkin, 'Plastic at the bottom of Mariana Trench', *The Ecologist*, 31 May 2019, theecologist.org/2019/may/31/plastic-bottom-mariana-trench (accessed 18 November 2022).

13 Philip Lymbery, *Sixty Harvests Left*, Bloomsbury Publishing, 2022.

14 Alesia M Jung et al., 'Excretion of polybrominated diphenyl ethers and AhR activation in breastmilk among firefighters', *Toxicological Sciences* 192(2), 28 February 2023, www.ncbi.nlm.nih.gov/pmc/articles/PMC10109531 (accessed 19 November 2023).

15 E Dewailly, A Nantel, JP Weber and F Meyer, 'High levels of PCBs in breast milk of Inuit women from arctic Quebec', US Department of Energy Office of Scientific and Technical Information, 1 November 1989, www.osti.gov/biblio/6614926 (accessed 18 November 2022).

16 Channel 4, 'What Killed the Whale?', broadcast 12 June 2022.

17 Arlene Blum, 'Killer couch chemicals', 17 November 2011, *Huffpost*, www.huffpost.com/entry/killer-couch-chemicals_b_60754 (accessed 18 November 2022).

18 WWF, 'Toxic chemicals a major threat to the Arctic', 1 October 2002, wwf.panda.org/wwf_news/?2694/Toxic-chemicals-a-major-threat-to-the-Arctic (accessed 18 November 2022).

19 H Dryden and D Duncan, 'Climate regulating ocean plants and animals are being destroyed by toxic chemicals and plastics, accelerating our path towards ocean pH 7.95 in 25 years which will devastate humanity', *Social Science Research Network*, 5 June 2021, www.papers.ssrn.com/sol3/papers.cfm?abstract_id=3860950 (accessed 18 November 2022).

20 Asad Rehman, 'A holistic approach to the multiple crisis', *Ethical Consumer conference*, 2019, www.ethicalconsumer.org/sites/default/files/inline-files/War%20on%20Want%20and%20ethical%20consumer%20%282%29.pdf (accessed 18 November 2022).

21 Jamie Hailstone, 'Paint is the largest source of microplastics in the ocean, study finds', *Forbes*, 9 February 2022, www.forbes.com/sites/jamiehailstone/2022/02/09/paint-is-the-largest-source-of-microplastics-in-the-ocean-study-finds/?sh=b96e4501dd80 (accessed 18 November 2022).

22 UN Environmental Programme, 'Why are coral reefs dying?', 12 November 2021, www.unep.org/news-and-stories/story/why-are-coral-reefs-dying (accessed 18 November 2022).

23 WWF, '69% average decline in wildlife populations since 1970, says new WWF report', 13 October 2022, www.worldwildlife.org/press-releases/69-average-decline-in-wildlife-populations-since-1970-says-new-wwf-report (accessed 18 November 2022).

24 Lindsey Stowell, 'The impact of diet on EU emissions', *Faunalytics*, 16 July 2022, www.faunalytics.org/the-impact-of-diet-on-e-u-emissions (accessed 18 November 2022).

25 Reuters, 'Humans may be eating a credit card's worth of plastic each week', 12 June 2019, www.reuters.com/article/us-environment-plastic-idUSKCN1TD009 (accessed 18 November 2022).

26 Greenpeace, 'Amazon rainforest', www.greenpeace.org.uk/challenges/forests/amazon-rainforest (accessed 18 November 2022).

27 World Health Organization, 'Drinking water', 21 March 2022, www.who.int/news-room/fact-sheets/detail/drinking-water (accessed 18 November 2022).

28 Sylvia Earle, Twitter/X, 2 November 2020, www.twitter.com/SylviaEarle/status/1323104408163426305?ref_src=twsrc%5Etfw%7Ctwcamp%5Etweetembed%7Ctwterm%5E1323104408163426305%7Ctwgr%5E46c7e1192731a55e008bcedbeb-1269c7c191a8c4%7Ctwcon%5Es1_c10&ref_url=https%3A%2F%2Fpublish.twitter.com%2F%3Fquery%3Dhttps3A2F2Ftwitter.com2FSylviaEarle2Fstatus2F-1323104408163426305widget%3DTweet (accessed 18 November 2022).

29 Andrew Simms, 'Earth Overshoot Day', New Economics Foundation, 2022, www.overshootday.org (accessed 18 October 2022).

30 REA Almond, M Grooten, D Juffe Bignoli and T Petersen (Eds), 'Living planet report 2022 – Building a naturepositive society', WWF, 2022.

Endnotes

31 Royal College of Art, 'Mykor start-up', 2022, www.rca.ac.uk/business/innovationrca/start-companies/mykor/#:~:text=World-wide%2C%20the%20construction%20indus-try%20contributes,and%2050%25%20of%20landfill%20waste (accessed 18 October 2022). Procure Partnerships Framework, 'How can we improve the negative impact construction has on the environment?', 13 May 2012, pro-curepartnerships.co.uk/how-can-we-improve-the-negative-impact-construction-has-on-the-environment (accessed 18 October 2022).

32 Matthew Lynch, 'Beyond sustainability: The story of a reformed capitalist', TEDx Honolulu, 5 March 2012, www.youtube.com/watch?v=-1qIXmusaeg8 (accessed 16 October 2023).

33 Dominique Hes, *Regenerative Development and Design: A Framework for Evolving Sustainability*, Wiley, 2016. See also www.regenesisgroup.com (accessed 18 October 2022).

34 B Corporations are businesses which commit to measuring, evaluating and improving to reduce their social and environmental impact. See also Chapter 11, Ethical Business.

35 William McDonough and Michael Braungart, *Cradle to Cradle: Remaking the Way We Make Things*, North Point Press, 2002, p 67.

36 Craig Welch, 'First study of all Amazon green-house gases suggests the damaged forest is now worsening climate change', *National Geographic*, 11 March 2021, www.nationalgeographic.com/environment/article/amazon-rainforest-now-ap-pears-to-be-contributing-to-climate-change (accessed 18 November 2022).

37 Drew Kann, 'The Amazon is a key buffer against climate change. A new study warns wildfires could decimate it', CNN, 10 January 2020, edition.cnn.com/2020/01/10/world/amazon-rain-forest-wildfires-climate-change-study/index.html (accessed 24 July 2023).

CHAPTER1

1 Graeme Brooker, 50|50 *Words for Reuse – A Minifesto*, Canalside Press, 2022.

2 Duncan Baker-Brown, *The Re-Use Atlas: A Designer's Guide Towards the Circular Economy*, RIBA Publishing 2024.

3 Hong Xinying, 'This secret new resort near Bangkok is a stylish ode to train travel', *Tatler Asia*, 13 July 2022, www.tatlerasia.com/homes/architecture-de-sign/intercontinental-khao-yai-resort-thai-land-bill-bensley-hotel-design (accessed 18 November 2022).

4 Bill Bensley, 'Sensible sustainable solutions', 2020, www.bensley.com/media/sensible-sustain-able-solutions (accessed 25 July 2023).

5 Hong Xinying, 'This Secret New Resort Near Bangkok Is a Stylish Ode to Train Travel,' Tatler Asia,www.tatlerasia.com/homes/architec-ture-design/intercontinental-khao-yai-resort-thai-land-bill-bensley-hotel-design> 13 July 2022 (accessed 18 November 2022)

6 Ulrike Rahe, 'Kitchen to cradle: Generating house-hold waste', *The Architectural Review*, 11 January 2022, www.architectural-review.com/essays/kitchen-to-cradle-generating-house-hold-waste (accessed 16 October 2023).

7 Paula Flores, 'Best kitchen appliances: How to buy the right items for your home', *Which?*, 28 June 2022, www.which.co.uk/reviews/fit-ted-kitchens/article/planning-a-kitchen/kitchen-ap-pliances-a8SJ78H7mSIA (accessed 18 November 2022).

8 Helen Lord, Used Kitchen Exchange, www.used-kitchenexchange.co.uk/how-does-it-work (accessed 18 November 2022). Rehome, 'FAQs: Is it a good idea to buy a used kitchen?', www.rehome.co.uk/kitchens (accessed 26 October 2023).

CHAPTER2

1 Brighton Permaculture Trust Green Architec-ture Day, 'Waste is a resource in the wrong place', 2 April 2015, www.youtube.com/watch?v=mRZ8Vo2fHeI (accessed 18 November 2022).

2 Ellen MacArthur Foundation, 'What is a circular economy?', www.ellenmacarthurfoundation.org/topics/circular-economy-introduction/overview (accessed 18 November 2022).

3 William McDonough and Michael Braungart, *The Upcycle: Beyond Sustainability – Designing for Abundance*, North Point Press, 2013, unnum-bered page before the contents page.

4 de Architekten Cie., *Lessons in Circularity*, 2021, www.cie.nl/ebook-circularity?lang=en (accessed 31 May 2023).

5 Quote provided to the author for this publication.

6 The Waste and Resources Action Programme, 'Study into the reuse potential of household bulky items', August 2012, www.wrap.org.uk/resources/report/study-re-use-potential-house-hold-bulky-items (accessed 16 December 2022).

7 UN News, 'Curb throw-away culture, says UN-Habitat chief, highlighting world day', 1 October 2018, www.news.un.org/en/sto-ry/2018/10/1021972 (accessed 24 October 2023).

8 Quote provided to the author for this publication.

9 RSA The Great Recovery, 'Rearranging the furniture – An RSA Great Recovery design residency in collaboration with SUEZ Recycling and Recovery UK', 2015.

10 Sophie Thomas, *Survivor Sofa Story Book*, 2015.

CHAPTER 3

1 Quote provided to the author for this publication.

2 James Wallman, *Stuffocation – Living More with Less*, Penguin Books, 2017.

3 Elinor Ochs and Tamar Kremer-Sadlik (Eds), *Fast-Forward Family: Home, Work and Relation-ships in Middle-Class America*, University of California Press, 2013.

4 Joshua Fields Millburn and Ryan Nicodemus, 'The Minimalists' podcast, Episode 251 – 'Stuffo-cated', 8 September 2020, www.youtube.com/watch?v=Esgi4GI2ceI (accessed 30 December 2022).

5 Jonathan Chapman, *Emotionally Durable Design: Objects, Experiences and Empathy*, Routledge, 2015.

6 Walter R Stahel, *The Circular Economy: A User's Guide*, Taylor & Francis, 2019.

7 Bauhaus Campus Berlin, 'Tiny Houses Meet Global Challenges', 2017–2018, http://bauhaus-campus.org/#campus (accessed 18 October 2023).

8 Quote provided to the author for this publication.

CHAPTER 4

1 Stephanie Feldstein, Emma Hakansson, Joshua Katcher and Unique Vance, 'Shear destruction: Wool, fashion and the biodiversity crisis', report for the Center for Biological Diversity and Collective Fashion Justice's CIRCUMFAUNA Initiative, November 2021, p 13.

2 Rachel Carson, *Silent Spring*, Houghton Mifflin, 1962.

3 United States Environmental Protection Agency (EPA), 'Human health issues related to pesticides', updated 17 October 2022, www.epa.gov/pesticide-science-and-assessing-pesticide-risks/human-health-issues-related-pesticides (accessed 20 April 2023).

4 Centers for Disease Control and Prevention, 'Dichlorodiphenyltrichloroethane (DDT) factsheet', 16 August 2021, www.cdc.gov/biomonitoring/DDT_FactSheet.html#:~:text=Print-,Dichlorodiphenyltrichloroethane%20(DDT),of%20mosquitoes%20that%20spread%20malaria (accessed 12 May 2023).

5 Untold Creative, *The True Cost*, documentary film, 2016, www.truecostmovie.com (accessed 12 July 2023).

6 Clare Carlile, 'Choosing the most sustainable fabric', *Ethical Consumer Magazine*, www.ethicalconsumer.org/fashion-clothing/choosing-most-sustainable-fabric (accessed 19 October 2023).

7 Fiona Harvey, 'Improving soil could keep world within 1.5C heating target, research suggests', *The Guardian*, 4 July 2023, www.theguardian.com/environment/2023/jul/04/improving-farming-soil-carbon-store-global-heating-target (accessed 12 July 2023).

8 WRAP, 'Citizen insights: Estimating the longevity of home textiles in the UK', April 2023, www.wrap.org.uk/resources/report/citizen-insights-estimating-longevity-home-textiles-uk#:~:text=Ownership%20%2D%20The%20average%20household%20in,two%20years%20longer%20than%20clothing (accessed 19 October 2023).

9 Quote provided to the author for this publication.

10 Radhika Sanghani, 'Stacey Dooley Investigates: Are your clothes wrecking the planet? "I feel like we understand what plastic does to the Earth but I had no idea what cotton was capable of"', BBC THREE, 9 October 2018, www.bbc.co.uk/bbcthree/article/5a1a43b5-cbae-4a42-8271-48f53b63bd07 (accessed 31 March 2023).

11 Elise Elsacker, Meng Zhang and Martyn Dade-Robertson, 'Fungal engineered living materials: The viability of pure mycelium materials with self-healing functionalities', *Advanced Functional Materials*, 11 April 2023, https://doi.org/10.1002/adfm.202301875 (accessed 20 April 2023).

12 World Wildlife Fund, 'Cork screwed? Environmental and economic impacts of the cork stoppers market', May 2006.

13 All information about the operational running of Burwood Brickworks was correct at time of opening; some adjustments have been implemented since this time, to ensure the centre is commercially and socially sustainable.

CHAPTER 5

1 'Vegan in British English', *Collins Dictionary*, www.collinsdictionary.com/dictionary/english/vegan (accessed 16 January 2023).

2 'Cruelty free in British English', Collins Dictionary, www.collinsdictionary.com/dictionary/english/cruelty-free (accessed 16 January 2023).

3 People for the Ethical Treatment of Animals (PETA), 'Environmental hazards of leather', www.peta.org/issues/animals-used-for-clothing/leather-industry/leather-environmental-hazards (accessed 27 January 2023).

4 Human Rights Watch, 'Toxic tanneries', 8 October 2012, www.hrw.org/report/2012/10/08/toxic-tanneries/health-repercussions-bangladeshs-hazaribagh-leather (accessed 27 January 2023).

5 PETA, 'Leather: Hell for animals and children in Bangladesh', www.headlines.peta.org/bangladesh-leather-exposed (accessed 27 January 2023).

6 Helen Farr-Leander, posted on LinkedIn.

7 Emma Hakansson and Joshua Katcher, 'The carbon cost of our leather goods, calculated', Collective Fashion Justice, January 2023, www.collectivefashionjustice.org/articles/carbon-cost-leather-goods (accessed 26 July 2023).

8 Leather Industry Data Shows Us It Is Far More Impactful Than Even Synthetic Alternatives'. Circumfauna. circumfauna.org/leather-carbon-footprint> (accessed 27 January 2023)

9 Circumfauna, 'Leather industry data shows us it is far more impactful than even synthetic alternatives', circumfauna.org/leather-carbon-footprint (accessed 27 January 2023).

10 PETA, 'The wool industry', https://www.peta.org/issues/animals-used-for-clothing/wool-industry (accessed 21 January 2023).

11 Quote provided to the author for this publication.

12 Humane Society International, 'Summer solstice dog meat eating begins in Yulin', 20 June 2022, https://www.hsi.org/news-media/yulin-dog-meat-festival (accessed 21 January 2023).

13 Alanna Weissman, 'Is your leather from China? It might be made of dog or cat skin', *The Guardian*, 31 July 2016, https://www.theguardian.com/business/2016/jul/31/dog-cat-leather-china-us-congress-trade-peta (accessed 21 January 2023).

14 Deborah DiMare, 'A Well-Designed Business'® podcast, episode 117, 'Cruelty-free design certification is here!', interview with LuAnn Nigara, https://luannnigara.com/117-power-talk-friday-deborah-rosenberg-cruelty-free-design-certification-is-here (accessed 21 January 2023).

15 Deborah DiMare, *Vegan Interiors*, Blurb, 2018.

16 Deborah DiMare, Vegan Interiors, Blurb, 20

17 Yvonne Taylor, PETA press release for PETA Vegan Homeware Awards, 2022, https://www.peta.org.uk/media/news-releases/john-lewis-dfs-and-aldi-among-winners-of-petas-2022-vegan-homeware-awards (accessed 30 October 2023).

18 Elisa Allen, PETA press release for PETA Vegan Homeware Awards, 2022, https://www.peta.org.uk/media/news-releases/john-lewis-dfs-and-aldi-among-winners-of-petas-2022-vegan-homeware-awards (accessed 30 October 2023).

CHAPTER 6

1 GoodWeave, *Hidden and Vulnerable Report*, 2020, https://goodweave.org/wp-content/uploads/2020/11/GoodWeave-Hidden-and-Vulnerable-Report-Final.pdf (accessed 31 March 2023).

2 Environmental Justice and Health Alliance for Chemical Policy Reform, *Who's in Danger? Race, Poverty and Chemical Disasters – A Democratic Analysis of Chemical Disaster Vulnerability Zones*, May 2014.

3 HBO Television, 'Toxic Hot Seat', television programme, release date 25 November 2013.

4 International Rescue Committee, '10 countries at risk of climate disaster', 10 March 2023, https://www.rescue.org/article/10-countries-risk-climate-disaster (accessed 31 March 2023).

5 Harriet Mercer, 'Colonialism: Why leading climate scientists have finally acknowledged its link with climate change', The Conversation, 22 April 2022, https://theconversation.com/colonialism-why-leading-climate-scientists-have-finally-acknowledged-its-link-with-climate-change-181642 (accessed 20 April 2023).

6 Irene San Segundo, 'Do you know how much garment workers really make?', Fashion Revolution, 2019, https://www.fashionrevolution.org/usa-blog/how-much-garment-workers-really-make/#:~:text=According%20to%20these%20brands%C2%B4,brands%20to%20do%20the%20same (accessed 31 May 2023).

Endnotes

7   Safia Minney, posted on LinkedIn.

8   Untold Creative, 'The True Cost', documentary film, USA, 2016, www.truecostmovie.com (accessed 28 July 2023).

9   Massachusetts Institute of Technology Senseable City Lab, 'Trash | Track' investigation, 2010, https://senseable.mit.edu/trashtrack (accessed 24 October 2023).

10 World Economic Forum, 'Every minute, one garbage truck of plastic is dumped into our oceans. This has to stop', 27 October 2016, https://www.weforum.org/agenda/2016/10/every-minute-one-garbage-truck-of-plastic-is-dumped-into-our-oceans (accessed 31 March 2023).

11 LADbible Group, Plastic Oceans and AMV BBDO, 'Trash Isles', 2018, https://www.youtube.com/watch?v=u9Ne9VnZ7fs (accessed 31 March 2023).

12 'Humans may be eating a credit card's worth of plastic each week', Reuters, 12 June 2019, https://www.reuters.com/article/us-environment-plastic-idUSKCN1TD009 (accessed 18 November 2022).

13 National Oceanic and Atmospheric Administration, US Department of Commerce, 'Ocean pollution and marine debris. Each year, billions of pounds of trash and other pollutants enter the ocean', 1 April 2020, https://www.noaa.gov/education/resource-collections/ocean-coasts/ocean-pollution#:~:text=The%20impact%20of%20marine%20pollution,food%20out%20of%20the%20water (accessed 31 October 2023).

14 UK Government, 'ENV23 – UK statistics on waste', 25 September 2014, updated 12 July 2022, https://www.gov.uk/government/statistical-data-sets/env23-uk-waste-data-and-management (accessed 31 March 2023).

15 Changing Streams, 'Changing streams calls on construction industry to join fight against plastic pandemic', https://www.changingstreams.org/changing-streams-calls-on-construction-industry-to-join-fight-against-plastic-pandemic (accessed 31 May 2023).

16 Quote provided to the author for this publication.

17 Goverment of the Netherlands, 'Government apologises for the Netherlands' role in the history of slavery', 19 October 2022, https://www.government.nl/latest/news/2022/12/19/government-apologises-for-the-netherlands-role-in-the-history-of-slavery (accessed 31 August 2023).

18 Quote provided to the author for this publication.

19 L Murphy, J Vallette and N Elimä, 'Built on repression: PVC building materials' reliance on labour and environmental abuses in the Uyghur region', Sheffield Hallam University Helena Kennedy Centre for International Justice, 2022.

20 US Department of Labor, 'List of goods produced by child labor or forced labor', 2022, https://www.dol.gov/agencies/ilab/reports/child-labor/list-of-goods#:~:text=The%20most%20common%20agricultural%20goods,and%20diamonds%20are%20most%20common (accessed 28 October 2023).

21 GoodWeave, 'Child labor', https://goodweave.org/the-issue (accessed 31 May 2023).

22 US Department of Labor, 'List of goods produced by child labor or forced labor'.

23 UNHCR, 'More than 100 million people are forcibly displaced', May 2022, https://www.unhcr.org/refugee-statistics/insights/explainers/100-million-forcibly-displaced.html#:~:text=More%20than%20100%20million%20people%20are%20forcibly%20displaced&text=At%20the%20end%20of%202021,flee%20stood%20at%2089.3%20million.&text=Since%20then%2C%20the%20war%20in,other%20countries%2C%20primarily%20in%20Europe (accessed 31 March 2023).

24 The Institute for Economics and Peace, The Ecological Threat Report 2022, October 2022, https://www.visionofhumanity.org/wp-content/uploads/2022/10/ETR-2022-Web-V1.pdf (accessed 31 May 2023).

1   REA Almond, M Grooten, D Juffe Bignoli and T Petersen (Eds), Living Planet Report 2022 – Building a Nature Positive Society, WWF, 2022.

CHAPTER 6

1   Charles Montgomery, Happy City – Transforming our Lives Through Urban Design, Penguin Books, 2013.

2   Ariane Thakore Ginwala, Wildlife Luxuries, 2023, https://wildlifeluxuries.com/our-story (accessed 26 October 2023).

3   Royal College of Art, 'Mykor', 2022, https://www.rca.ac.uk/business/innovationrca/start-companies/mykor/#:~:text=World-wide%2C%20the%20construction%20industry%20contributes,and%2050%25%20of%20landfill%20waste (accessed 18 October 2022). Procure Partnerships Framework, 'How Can we

Improve the Negative Impact Construction has on the Environment?', 13 May 2012, https://procurepartnerships.co.uk/how-can-we-improve-the-negative-impact-construction-has-on-the-environment (accessed 18 October 2022).

CHAPTER 8

1   Sylvia Earle, tweet on Twitter/X, 20 June 2022, https://twitter.com/SylviaEarle/status/1539019359057653760 (accessed 29 October 2023).

2   Stephen Kellert and Elizabeth Calabrese, The Practice of Biophilic Design, 2015, https://www.biophilic-design.com (accessed 26 October 2023).

3   Terrapin Bright Green, 14 Patterns of Biophilic Design, Improving Health and Wellbeing in the Built Environment, https://www.terrapinbrightgreen.com/report/14-patterns (accessed 4 January 2023).

4   Niranjika Wijesooriya and Arianna Brambilla, 'Bridging biophilic design and environmentally sustainable design: A critical review', Journal of Cleaner Production 283, 2021.

5   United Nations Population Fund, 'State of world population 2007', 1 January 2007, https://www.unfpa.org/publications/state-world-population-2007 (accessed 4 January 2023).

6   Katie Hill, 'An epidemic of climate anxiety', My Green Pod, 21 March 2023, https://www.mygreenpod.com/articles/an-epidemic-of-climate-anxiety (accessed 23 March 2023).

7   Tara John, 'Doctors are prescribing nature to patients in the UK's Shetland Islands', CNN, 5 October 2018, https://edition.cnn.com/2018/10/05/health/nature-prescriptions-shetland-intl/index.html (accessed 15 March 2023).

8   Linda Geddes, Chasing the Sun, Wellcome Collection, 2019.

9   Linda Geddes 'What I learned living without artificial light', BBC Future, 25 April 2018, https://www.bbc.com/future/article/20180424-what-i-learnt-by-living-without-artificial-light (accessed 26 October 2023).

10 Omid Kardan, Peter Gozdyra, Bratislav Misic, Faisal Moola, Lyle J Palmer, Tomáš Paus and Marc G Berman, 'Neighborhood greenspace and health in a large urban center', Scientific Reports, 9 July 2015, https://www.nature.com/articles/srep11610 (accessed 19 March 2023).

11 Florence Nightingale, Notes on Hospitals, Longman, Green, Longman, Roberts and Green, 1863.

12 Florence Nightingale, 'Letter from Florence Nightingale describing the benefits of clean air', 8 September 1860, https://www.bl.uk/collection-items/letter-from-florence-nightingale-describing-the-benefits-of-clean-air (accessed 19 March 2023).

13 Roger S Ulrich, 'View through a window may influence recovery from surgery', *Science* **224**, 27 April 1984, https://www.researchgate.net/publication/17043718_View_Through_a_Window_May_Influence_Recovery_from_Surgery (accessed 19 March 2023).

14 Health and Safety Executive, 'Work-related stress, anxiety or depression statistics in Great Britain, 2022 data up to March 2022, annual statistics', 23 November 2022.

15 S Gritzka, TE MacIntyre, D Dörfel, JL Baker-Blanc and G Calogiuri, 'The effects of workplace nature-based interventions on the mental health and well-being of employees: A systematic review', *Front Psychiatry* **28**, April 2020, https://www.ncbi.nlm.nih.gov/pmc/articles/PMC7198870 (accessed 31 May 2023).

16 International Living Future Institute, The Living Building Challenge^SM course, 'Getting started in biophilic design' module.

17 Amanda Sturgeon, International Living Future Institute, 'Using biophilic design to heal mind, body and soul', TED MED 2018, https://www.tedmed.com/talks/show?id=729937 (accessed 29 October 2023).

18 OPN Architects, 'Marion Fire Station 1', https://opnarchitects.com/portfolio/marion-fire-station-headquarters (accessed 18 June 2023).

19 Danielle Brooker, 'Choosing to burn out on your terms and how to find your calm', *Forbes* magazine, 22 March 2019, https://www.forbes.com/sites/daniellebrooker/2019/03/22/women-in-wellness-burn-out-on-your-terms-how-to-find-your-calm (accessed 18 June 2023).

20 Elora Hardy, 'Bali: Sharma Springs', series 1, episode 3 of 'Home', Apple TV +, 17 April 2020.

21 William McDonough and Michael Braungart, *Cradle to Cradle: Remaking the Way We Make Things*, North Point Press, 2002.

22 Quote provided to the author for this publication.

23 PEFC (Programme for the Endorsement of Forest Certification), 'Introduction to the Brazilian Forest Certification System', 18 July 2022, https://www.youtube.com/watch?v=4WAarlHaedI (accessed 23 June 2023).

24 Guto Requena, *Hybrid Dwelling: Subjectivities and Home Architecture in the Digital Age*, Senac SP, 2019.

CHAPTER 9

1 Alison Mears, Healthier Materials and Sustainable Building course, The New School – Parsons School of Design, April 2022, https://www.newschool.edu/parsons/healthier-materials-sustainable-building-certificate (accessed 30 October 23).

2 NHS for England, 'Sick building syndrome', 22 September 2020, https://www.nhs.uk/conditions/sick-building-syndrome (accessed 20 March 2023).

3 Umwelt Bundesamt, 'Chemicals: Better protection of environment and health; steady increase of chemicals use worldwide', 30 November 2021, https://www.umweltbundesamt.de/en/press/pressinformation/chemicals-better-protection-of-environment-health (accessed 30 March 2023).

4 Brighton and Hove City Council, 'Improving air quality and tackling pollution for Clean Air Day', 16 June 2022, https://www.brighton-hove.gov.uk/news/2022/improving-air-quality-and-tackling-pollution-clean-air-day (accessed 16 February 2023).

5 Allergy UK, 'Indoor air quality' factsheet, 18 June 2022, https://www.allergyuk.org/resources/indoor-air-quality-factsheet (accessed 30 October 23).

6 Green Science Policy Institute, 'PFAS in building materials', https://greensciencepolicy.org/our-work/building-materials/pfas-in-building-materials (accessed 16 February 2023).

7 Anna S Young, Nicholas Herkert, Heather M Stapleton, Brent A Coull, Russ Hauser, Thomas Zoeller, Peter A Behnisch, Emiel Felzel, Abraham Brouwer and Joseph G Allen, 'Hormone receptor activities of complex mixtures of known and suspect chemicals in personal silicone wristband samplers worn in office buildings', *Chemosphere* **315**, 2023, https://www.sciencedirect.com/science/article/pii/S0045653522041984 (accessed 20 March 2023).

8 International Living Future Institute, 'About the Red List', https://living-future.org/red-list (accessed 20 March 2023).

9 UK Hempcrete, 'Will Stanwix and Kevin McCloud on low-tech vs high-tech materials', Grand Designs Live, May 2013, https://www.youtube.com/watch?v=DO8H1imZtEA (accessed 20 March 2023).

10 Bob King, 'Path sustainable office chair', Humanscale, 26 March 2023, https://uk.humanscale.com/path/sustainabilityV2.cfm (accessed 31 October 2023).

CHAPTER 10

1 International Monetary Fund, 'One-on-one with Christine Lagarde, featuring Sir David Attenborough: Balancing Nature and the Global Economy', 11 April 2019, https://meetings.imf.org/en/2019/Spring/Schedule/2019/04/11/imf-seminar-one-on-one-lagarde (accessed 24 May 2023).

2 Hannah Ritchie, 'How much of the world's food production is dependent on pollinators?', Our World in Data, 2 August 2021, https://ourworldindata.org/pollinator-dependence (accessed 24 May 2023).

3 Rachel Carson, *Silent Spring*, Houghton Mifflin, 1962.

4 Richard Gregory, 'Europe has lost over half a billion birds in 40 years. The single biggest cause? Pesticides and fertilisers', The Conversation, 1 June 2023, https://theconversation.com/europe-has-lost-over-half-a-billion-birds-in-40-years-the-single-biggest-cause-pesticides-and-fertilisers-206826? (accessed 2 June 2023).

5 REA Almond, M Grooten, D Juffe Bignoli and T Petersen (Eds), *Living Planet Report 2022 – Building a Nature Positive Society*, WWF, 2022.

6 Global Monitoring Laboratory, 'Trends in atmospheric carbon dioxide – Mauna Loa, Hawaii', https://gml.noaa.gov/ccgg/trends/mlo.html (accessed 31 May 2023).

7 World Green Building Council, 'Bringing embodied carbon upfront', 2019, https://worldgbc.org/advancing-net-zero/embodied-carbon/#:~:text=Buildings%20are%20currently%20responsible%20for,11%25%20from%20materials%20and%20construction (accessed 18 June 2023).

8 Quote provided to the author for this publication

9 Duncan Baker-Brown, 'Can architecture matter?', TEDxBrighton,

https://www.youtube.com/watch?v=k-WUpV6J1JN8 (accessed 11 July 2023).

10 Philip Lymbery, *Sixty Harvests Left*, Bloomsbury Publishing, 2022.

11 Fiona Harvey, 'Improving soil could keep world within 1.5C heating target, research suggests', *The Guardian*, 4 July 2023, https://www.theguardian.com/environment/2023/jul/04/improving-farming-soil-carbon-store-global-heating-target (accessed 12 July 2023).

12 Soil Association, 'Help save our green and pleasant land from poisonous pesticides', https://www.soilassociation.org/causes-campaigns/help-us-protect-our-wildlife-from-pesticides (accessed 26 October 2023).

Endnotes

13 X Sun, C Liddicoat, A Tiunov *et al.*, 'Harnessing soil biodiversity to promote human health in cities', 14 February 2023, https://doi.org/10.1038/s42949-023-00086-0 (accessed 24 July 2023).

14 WWF, 'Deforestation and forest degradation', https://www.worldwildlife.org/threats/deforestation-and-forest-degradation#:~:text=Deforestation%20and%20forest%20degradation%20are,-frequency%20of%20extreme%20weather%20events (accessed 18 June 2023).

15 US Customs and Border Protection, 'Illegal logging', 30 November 2022, https://www.cbp.gov/trade/programs-administration/natural-resources-protection/illegal-logging (accessed 18 June 2023).

16 Preferred By Nature, 'What is illegal logging?', https://www.preferredbynature.org/sourcinghub/info/illegal-logging-0 (accessed 11 July 2023).

17 European Commission, 'Hemp production in the EU', https://agriculture.ec.europa.eu/farming/crop-productions-and-plant-based-products/hemp_en (accessed 18 June 2023).

18 Anita Roddick, *Business As Unusual*, Anita Roddick Books, 2005.

CHAPTER 11

1 Safia Minney, posted on LinkedIn.

2 Quote provided to the author for this publication.

3 Quote provided to the author for this publication.

4 Anita Roddick, *Business As Unusual*, Anita Roddick Books, 2005.

5 Anita Roddick, *Body and Soul*, Vermillion, 1992.

6 B Corporation, 'United Kingdom, Company Limited by Shares Legal Requirement', https://www.bcorporation.net/en-us/legal-requirement/country/united-kingdom/corporate-structure/company-limited-by-shares (accessed 31 March 2023).

7 Business & IP Centre London, 'Anita Roddick, part 1 (Inspiring Entrepreneurs – Commerce with a Conscience)', 15 November 2006, https://www.youtube.com/watch?v=iJ3THkgcSeo (accessed 31 March 2023).

8 'Greenhouse gas emissions are categorised into three groups or "scopes" by the most widely used international accounting tool, the Greenhouse Gas (GHG) Protocol. While scope 1 and 2 cover direct emissions sources (eg fuel used in company vehicles and purchased electricity), scope 3 emissions cover all indirect emissions due to the activities of an organisation,' edie Jargon Buster, www.edie.net/definition/scope-emissions (accessed 30 October 2023).

Index

Index

Index

Image Credits

Illustrations on ppVI-IX, XIV, 18, 34, 50, 64, 78, 90, 108, 124, 138, 152 by Elena Branch @elenadrewthis

Figure 1.1, 1.2 Bill Bensley; 1.3, 1.4, 1.5, 1.6 InterContinental Khao Yai Resort; 1.7, 1.8, 1.9, 1.10, 1.11, 1.12, 1.13, 1.14 Mecanoo; 1.15, 1.16, 1.17, 1.18 NOSIGNER; 1.19 Patricia Semir, 2021, reproduced by permission of Casa Décor; 1.20, 1.22 more&co; 1.21 Nacho Uribesalazar, 2021, reproduced by permission of Casa Décor; 2.1, 2.2, 2.4, 2.5, 2.6, 2.7, 2.8, 2.9 ABN AMRO; 2.3 ABN AMRO. Photo: Egbert De Boer Fotografie; 2.10, 2.11, 2.12, 2.13, 2.14 Urselmann Interior. Photo: Magdalena Gruber; 2.15, 2.16, 2.17, 2.18 Ella Doran; 3.1, 3.2, 3.3 ZZ Driggs; 3.4, 3.5, 3.6a-c NOSIGNER; 3.7 Lynton Pepper, Architecture 00; 3.8 Photo: Rory Gardiner; 3.9, 3.10, 3.11, 3.12, 3.13 Photo: Jake Balston; 4.1, 4.2, 4.3 Two Sisters Ecotextiles; 4.4 Luca Alessandrini; 4.5, 4.6 DAM & André Rocha; 4.7, 4.8, 4.9, 4.10, 4.11, 4.12, 4.13 Frasers Property Australia; 5.1 Hilton London Bankside; 5.2, 5.3 Saosa 1875; 5.4, 5.5 Veshin Factory International Ltd; 5.6, 5.7, 5.8, 5.9, 5.10, 5.11 DiMare Design; 5.12 Faborg; 6.1 Selyn Textiles; 6.2 PaperTale; 6.3, 6.4, 6.5 Netherlands Embassy; 6.6 © UNHCR / U. Jagannathan; 6.7 © UNHCR / B Barb; 6.8 GoodWeave International; 6.9 Love Welcomes; 7.1, 7.2, 7.3, 7.4 Photo: Christopher Frederick Jones; 7.5, 7.6, 7.7, 7.8, 7.9 Photo: Ishita Sitwala; 7.10 Photo: Meister Meister; 7.11, 7.12, 7.13, 7.16, 7.17 Mario Cucinella Architects; 7.14 Mario Cucinella Architects. Photo: Enrico Sua' Ummarino, Sawaya & Moroni; 7.15 Mario Cucinella Architects. Photo: Lago Corazza; 7.18 Photo: Ace & Tate; 7.19, 7.20 StoneCycling®; 7.21 Tom van Soest; 8.1, 8.2, 8.3, 8.4 Photo: Re:mind Studio; 8.5, 8.7, 8.8, 8.9, 8.10, 8.11 IBUKU. Photo: Rio Helmi; 8.6 IBUKU. Photo: Errol Vaes; 8.12, 8.14, 8.15, 8.16 Estudio Guto Requena. Photo: Maíra Acayaba; 8.13 Estudio Guto Requena. Photo: Fran Parente; 9.1, 9.3, 9.4, 9.5, 9.6 Photo: William Geddes; 9.2 Photo: Jonsara Ruth; 9.7 Photo: Anne Schlecter; 9.8, 9.9, 9.10, 9.11 Photo: Andy Harris for HG Matthews; 9.12 HumanScale Photo: Jeremy Frechette; 9.13 HumanScale; 10.1, 10.2, 10.3 Mark Waghorn Design; 10.4 Photo: Dillion Marsh; 10.5, 10.6 HempWood; 10.7, 10.12, 10.13 Vestre. Photo: Einar Aslaksen; 10.8, 10.10, 10.11 Vestre. Photo: Nicolas Tourrenc; 10.9 Viktoria Millentrup. Photo: Annika Weertz; 11.1, 11.2, 11.3 Nichloas Sangaré; 11.4 skinflint; 11.5, 11.6, 11.7, 11.8 skinflint. Photo: Elliott White; 11.9, 11.10, 11.11, 11.12, 11.13 Photo: The Body Shop International.